MAKE NO SMALL PLANS
THE UNIVERSITY OF CALGARY AT FORTY

Anthony Rasporich

Thank you for all your
efforts on behalf of the
U of C

[signature]

In appreciation of
your service as a Senator
of the University of Calgary
and in anticipation of
a relationship that
will continue into the future,
Warm regards,
Joanne Cuthbertson

UNIVERSITY OF
CALGARY

Library and Archives Canada Cataloguing in
Publication

Rasporich, Anthony W., 1940-
    Make no small plans : the University of Calgary at
forty / Anthony
Rosporich.

Includes bibliographical references and index.
ISBN 978-0-88953-315-8

    1. University of Calgary—History. I. Title.

LE3.C32R38 2007   378.7123'38
C2006-907046-6

∞ Printed in Canada by Houghton Boston
on Rolland Enviro 100 Edition Text acid free paper
Cover and interior design by Mieka West
Inside front/back cover photos by David Brown

TABLE OF CONTENTS

"Calgary Civic Centre as It May
Appear Many Years Hence" 1913.
Canadian Architectural Archives, University
of Calgary, Accession 14A/77.87

Make no small plans. They have no magic to stir humanity's blood and probably themselves will not be realized. Make big plans, aim high in hope and work, remembering that a noble, logical plan once recorded will never die,

But long after we are gone will be a living thing, asserting itself with ever-growing insistency. Remember that our sons and daughters are going to do things that will stagger us. Let your watchword be order and your beacon, beauty. Think big.

This vision of urban planning by the noted American architect, Daniel Burnham of Chicago, at the turn of the twentieth century, could well describe the vision of the city of Calgary's founders, who in 1912 commissioned Thomas Mawson, a British architect and visionary urban planner to develop a master plan for development. Where Burnham had conjured up a Chicago that was a "Paris on the Prairie," Mawson envisioned a "Vienna on the Bow," a City Beautiful that included a private university. Sadly, the Mawson Plan for Calgary soon foundered in the depression that preceded World War I. Nonetheless, the dream of a university was sustained throughout three decades of stagnation, depression, and war, until in 1947 the Leduc oil discovery flooded the province with revenues from its abundant natural resources. The visionary spirit of Mawson burned bright once more, and the dream for a university for Calgary began to be realized; first, in the modest outbuildings on the SAIT campus, and then in two inauspicious buildings on the west end of the city. That humble beginning in the prairie dustbowl of 1960 was transformed into the North Hill campus, a small city unto itself serving close to thirty thousand students. The story of those who built it is told here.

ACKNOWLEDGEMENTS

No book can be seen as an individual enterprise, and this one, more than most, is a collective effort. I was asked last December by the Vice President (Academic) to provide input to a fortieth anniversary committee chaired by Kara Exner, and including Don Smith (History), and Terry Reilly (Archives). The committee was interested in a memoir of the university's first forty years. We explored ways of establishing oral interviewing as a means of exciting communal memories and then integrating these into a narrative of the university since it gained autonomy in 1966. We also determined that no hard-and-fast categories should exclude the formative years before 1960.

We then set about completing the first phase of interviews, and were fortunate to secure on short notice a professional interviewer, Tim Christison, who once worked for Com Media, and is well known for her work in media and theatre in Calgary. She set about her task with enthusiasm, and with foreknowledge of many of the characters and the story of the university during these past forty years. Like many, I was also the recipient of the generosity of Don Smith, who shared with me his historical files on the university. Last, I received the wonderful cooperation of Terry Reilly and the university archives staff, Lisa Atkinson, Suzanne Ell, Jennifer Willard, and Apollonia Steele of Special Collections, who provided me with the photos and documents that illustrate this book.

Many contributed their reminiscences, both past and present, and helped move this book along, not only by granting interviews, but also by passing on personal materials to illustrate this work. Finley Campbell donated some valuable memorabilia, addresses, and memoirs of his many years here, as did Peter Krueger, Bill Cochrane, Marsha Hanen, Bob Weyant, Mary Valentich, Roger Jackson, John Heintz, Gary Krivy, Vern Jones, Mike McMordie, and many others of the interviewees. All gave of their time generously and while I was not able to use all of their shared thoughts and memories, the tapes form a legacy of their working life here and will be preserved for posterity. It is a start along the road towards a full history of this remarkable institution, which in a short few decades finds itself in the enviable position of being in the top ten research universities in Canada.

After an interview phase of four months, I found myself in the unenviable position of having to produce this memoir of the university in six short weeks. I was helped not only by the recall of those who forged this institution but also by the historical record of their participation. The campus newspapers of the day offered a weekly record of events – a historical context – as did the minutes of GFC and its committees. The student newspaper, the *Gauntlet,* also was an invaluable source.

Finally, I should like to express my thanks to those members of my family and my friends who patiently waited while I completed this work. This time, although brief, was intensive. As always, the errors and interpretations of this story are peculiarly my own, and despite the best intentions of others, I can say that I alone am responsible for this version of the remarkable story of a university in the making.

A.W. Rasporich
Calgary, July 2006.

CHAPTER 1

BIRTH AND REBIRTH: THE FIRST SIXTY YEARS

CALGARY COLLEGE AND BEYOND: 1906–46

Although Calgary failed to become the provincial capital in 1905, it continued to have hopes of securing the site for a new provincial university. When the decision came down that year to locate it in the Strathcona riding of the provincial premier, A.C. Rutherford, considerable political protest and pressure were exerted against adoption of the northern site. It was of no avail; instead, Calgary received the Alberta Normal School for teacher training the following year.[1] Despite this setback, Calgarians persisted, and through their MLA, R.B. Bennett, presented a petition to the provincial legislature in 1910.[2] Bennett was able to push an act through the legislature incorporating Calgary College. It lacked, however, crucial provisions to allow the college to grant degrees and to control examinations governing admissions to the learned professions.

The events of the next four years were an exercise in pure frustration. Two attempts were made in the legislature to achieve university status, and both failed. The college's financial backers in the community continued to raise funds through its board chair, Dr. Thomas Blow, and other board members such as R.B. Bennett, H. W. Riley, and W.J. Tregillus.[3] They raised an impressive $400,000 with further

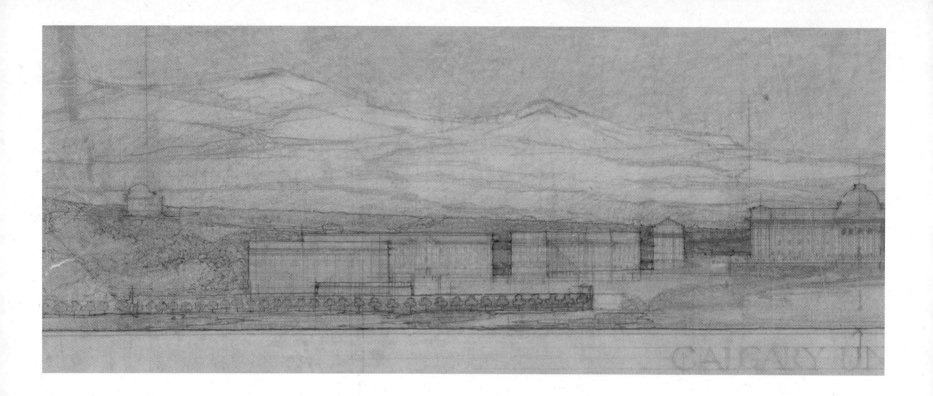

promises of $1 million, and secured a square mile of land from William Tregillus in Strathcona, a tract twice the size of the University of Alberta site in Edmonton.

The city, for its part, was committed to $150,000 for a building to house the new Faculty of Arts. Dr. Blow proudly asserted, "Give me land, and I'll build a university."[4] Indeed, new faculty were soon hired – five distinguished professors in the arts and a law department with thirteen part-time members – and classes were slated for the downtown Carnegie Library. The college's board commissioned a Toronto architectural firm, Dunnington-Grubb, to draft a grand plan for the university campus in Strathcona Park. This campus plan drew upon the Oxford and Cambridge ideal of a university, replete with Gothic buildings, and housing new faculties, student dormitories, and a dining hall. Resolutely, and with prophetic irony, the new Dean of Arts, Dr. Edward Braithwaite, remarked, "It may take 50 years, but it will be done."[5]

At the height of the boom in 1912, Braithwaite and his colleagues fashioned a full curriculum for the session commencing October 1 at Calgary College. Student fees were ten dollars for the half year, and fees for single courses were three. Students and staff, over sixty in all, proudly posed on the steps of the Carnegie Library, anticipating an auspicious future for higher education in the burgeoning city of 40,000.[6] But the boom began to slow and by 1913 signs of a bust and a deepening recession were evident.

Despite repeated attempts to persuade the government to allow degree-granting status and an unfettered charter, it seemed, as Calgary MLA S.B. Hillcocks noted, that the policy of the government was "seriously and needlessly handicapping the efforts of public-spirited citizens and those in search of higher education."[7] It was increasingly difficult to keep Calgary College going in the 1913–14 academic year. Dr. Braithwaite resigned, and Dr. F.M. MacDougall took over as

acting dean, hiring a promising young historian, Walter N. Sage, as a replacement for Braithwaite.[8] Still, the college expanded, and the city and the college kept up the political pressure, announcing that a $150,000 building would be constructed, first to house classrooms and later to be refitted as a dormitory for the students.[9]

Under the never-ending pressure from the southern city, the Liberal government appointed a commission in October of 1914, headed by Robert Falconer, president of the University of Toronto, and two other university presidents, Arthur Stanley Mackenzie from Dalhousie, and Walter Murray from Saskatoon.[10] Their report in late December 1914 recommended yet again that degree-granting powers not be given to Calgary. There was, however, a new concession that an Institute of Technology be established in Calgary, to be supported and controlled jointly with the province.[11] It was unlikely that the commission would have decided otherwise. In line with University of Alberta President Henry Marshall Tory, these presidents agreed that a single university in each province was best.

Calgary was thus left with only the preliminary excavations at the Strathcona Hill site, still visible forty years later. When Calgary College closed its doors in 1915, there were also debts of some $10,000 in civic loans and nearly $6,000 in operating expenses. It had been, as Walter Sage wrote in his memoir of the "real estate university," an idealistic, somewhat utopian attempt at a privately-funded university in the prewar boom.[12] The Provincial Institute of Technology and Art (PITA) struggled on until the middle of the Great War, when it was taken over by the Department of Soldiers' Civil Re-Establishment as a hospital. In the pandemic of 1918, it operated as a flu hospital, and was revived as a technical school in 1921 under the auspices of the United Farmers of Alberta, gradually emerging as a vital source of post-secondary technical and art education.[13]

At the same time, the Calgary Normal School of 1906 had expanded its operations under its principal, E.W. Coffin (1911–1940), and was looking to expand its teacher training to two years. In the twenties, it moved to share a building with the Technical Institute on the North Hill campus, taking over eight classrooms on the west end of the building and offering university courses in education and psychology

The faculty and students of the University of Calgary, October 4, 1912 at commencement of fall classes. The group is assembled on the steps of the Calgary Public Library. Faculty in front row are left to right: F.H. McDougall, Mack Eastman, Dean E.A. Braithwaite, Cr. F.C. Ward, and Librarian Alex Calhoun. Glenbow Archives, NA 713-1.

Southern Alberta Institute of Technology, later Wireless School during World War Two.

from the University of Alberta as part of its extension program.[14] Arts students could also enroll at Mount Royal, a privately-funded Methodist college founded by the Reverend George Kerby in 1910.[15] In 1931, it became affiliated with the University of Alberta, offering first-year arts and science classes. Although the three institutions offered a mixture of technical and arts education, only partial or basic career paths at best were available to Calgary's post-secondary students of the interwar period.

For the rest of the Depression years, there were few opportunities to press the provincial government for changes to post-secondary education, as the Social Credit government teetered on the edge of bankruptcy and Calgary narrowly avoided insolvency as well. In this bleak fiscal climate, the status quo of a first year at Mount Royal affiliated with the University of Alberta, the PITA, or the Normal School, was not only a necessary limitation, but a welcome one.

REBIRTH: CALGARY BRANCH AND UNIVERSITY OF ALBERTA IN CALGARY, 1945–60

World War II changed everything. A wartime economy, increases in urbanization, and the deferred expectations of a rising population of veteran soldiers after the war all fueled a shift in public attitude. As early as 1942, the University of Alberta Survey Committee tabled its interim report to the Alberta legislature recommending expansion of the Normal School and the Technical School to a two-year program. Mount Royal College proposed to initiate an intake of first-year engineering students in the fall of 1943, and it continued to press for expansion of its former legal affiliation with the University of Alberta to the end of the second year.[16] The Calgary Normal School then became a part of the Faculty of Education of the University of Alberta on April 1, 1945, while the buildings continued under the operation of the Department of Public Works. At that time, 145 students were admitted to the first year, although only 16 were going the B.Ed. route.

Calgary's citizenry continued to agitate for a second-year program. Five hundred attended a meeting on February 13, 1946 chaired by William Reid, Superintendent of Education for the Calgary Public School Board, to demand second-year teacher training, first-year arts and science, and steps to establish a complete branch of the University of Alberta in Calgary.[17] On the following day, a resolution calling for the establishment of a Calgary branch was presented to the school boards, indicating support from all communities and school divisions in southern Alberta. By early 1946, the Calgary Branch waded into the fray with its own petitions, a standing committee of the city council, and the more broadly based Calgary University Committee (CUC). In March, the Calgary Branch staff was told that arrangements were being made for a limited second year of the B.Ed. and that lecture and lab space would be expanded on the Tech grounds.[18]

All eyes turned to Edmonton for further concessions towards university courses and expansion of the Calgary Branch, but both President Newton and Dean Lazerte at the University of Alberta indicated that these would have to be postponed due to costs. The Social Credit premier, Ernest Manning, reinforced this message through his minister of education. He explained that the government rejected petitions for a degree-granting institution because it was "quite clear that the decentralization of the university facilities results in a considerable duplication in both staff and equipment."[19] The premier further remarked that postwar enrolment would not sustain itself in Calgary, and that Edmonton could easily meet the demand for post-secondary education; hence, a second university was not warranted.[20]

This outright refusal merely spurred on the political pressure from Calgary. The CUC tried to persuade the city to set aside land on which to build a university in Hounsfield Heights, southwest of the Tech campus and in response, these lands were traded by the city for 200 acres on the Bennett and Downie estates further to the west to be held for a university campus if and when government approval was granted.

The major oil discoveries at Leduc in February of 1947 greatly expanded the Alberta economy for the ensuing decades. That same year, Calgary was granted branch status, arts and science courses were expanded for B.Ed. students, and the second-year teacher-training courses were officially announced. Arrangements were immediately made to borrow teachers from the Calgary Board to offer first-year courses such as chemistry, English, French, history and mathematics in Arts and Science. Andrew Doucette, Calgary Branch director, initiated a search for permanent or regular full-time staff.One of the first hired for the fall of 1948 was Dr. George M. Self, a historian and graduate of McGill and Chicago, who assumed teaching duties in history and political economy. With further increases in staff, pressures increased to secure local autonomy for Calgary Faculty Council, and Dr. Self led the charge for amendment of the University Act.[21] However, all that happened was that the University of Alberta sent agendas of its meetings two weeks earlier to Calgary, allowing time for Calgary's faculty to meet, and to discuss and forward resolutions to Edmonton. If necessary, Calgary faculty also travelled to Edmonton. Self forced his aging 1942 Cadillac, "Agatha," up the old Highway 2 at speeds well in excess of posted limits. For those faculty and occasional students brave enough to share a ride, the difficulties of branch-plant status were most evident.

Other barriers also impeded normal development, since course organization, examination grading, and posting of final marks were all planned in Edmonton. The most mundane tasks – compiling reading lists and making book orders – could not be done without approval from a distance. Local teachers could not reveal marks to their students without approval from the Registrar at the University of Alberta, nor could a student admission be processed without first going to Edmonton for official approval. In addition, the original sixteen students in the B.Ed. program, among them Ethel King-Shaw, later the first woman to attain a full professorship at the U of C, found themselves "taking a horrendous number of courses to complete the B.Ed. requirements." [22]

Small wonder, then, that Calgary enrolments declined in the late forties. Teaching was losing the lustre it once held, increasingly perceived as a profession with no future.[23] The infrastructural support so evident in Edmonton for courses in arts and sciences was lacking. There were only six regular areas: English, French, history, political economy, mathematics, and chemistry. Calgarians would have to wait until 1951 to be able to enter the first year of the B.A., B.Sc., B.Sc. in Nursing, or course work leading to Medicine, Law and Dentistry. There was, as well, an identity issue related to sharing facilities at the Tech. In the irreverent words of the student newspaper, the *Calvette*, "One third of the Calgary population thinks that the university is in Mount Royal, another third thinks the university is part of the Tech, and ... the rest never heard of it."[24] Enrolments only inched forward from 200 to 250 full-time students, and then to a modest 350 (250 in Education, 100 in Arts and Science, including Commerce and Nursing) plus 650 part-time students by the mid-fifties. Rumors began to circulate among the students that the future looked dim for the fledgling branch, and that the B.Ed. program might be closed down in 1955.[25] Even President Stewart of the University of Alberta chided Calgarians, stating that "Calgary has not given the support it should have done to the Branch here, much to the disappointment of the Board of Governors."

Calgary's civic leaders sprang into action. In 1955, the city council, at the prompting of Alderman Grant MacEwan, a great believer in higher education, pressed for a further commitment to a larger site for campus construction. Calgary City Council passed a resolution in September approving a ninety-nine-year lease of 348 acres at one dollar, with an option to purchase. In 1956, President Stewart and Calgary solicitor Edward Bredin agreed upon a thirty-year lease for one dollar a month, with a purchase option when a suitable building was built, adequate to house all courses. Once the deal was approved, the University of Alberta proposed a name change from the Calgary Branch to The University of Alberta in Calgary (UAC). In 1958, the government approved two buildings to be started in 1959: one for Education, Liberal Arts and Administration, and another for Science, Engineering, and Food Services. Both were to be built within three years.[26]

By June of 1958, a second year was added to Engineering, the department having initiated a first year in 1957. A first year in Commerce, Nursing, Arts and Science, and courses leading to Medicine and Dentistry, and a third and fourth year in Education would begin at the new campus. By October of 1958, a model of the long-term development was unveiled by the Department of Public Works at Calgary City Council. It was anticipated that the first stage would accommodate 1,000 full-time students. It was also proposed that Physical Education, introduced as a program in 1956, would receive a building, followed in sequence by a library building, a building for Education, and a student residence.[27]

A sod-turning dedication was arranged for November 1, 1958. This was largely to give hope to those thirty-four faculty members and students who had been toiling in less than ideal conditions, some for months and some for a matter of years. Fred

Terentiuk, who had come to teach physics in the fall of 1958, was sent out to the Banff Trail site with Dave Armstrong of Chemistry.

> Our job was to go out there and find a route … by which a busload of people could get to a nice spot where the sod could be turned to basically initiate the University of Calgary campus. Dave and I did this, and several days before the sod turning we went out and loosened up the soil in a way that was unobtrusive, and soaked it down so it was good and soft, and then marked it with a piece of paper, and a eight-inch spike, and marked out a route. And

SAIT Campus, 1958. Students' Union building. UC 85.025.01.22

Andy Doucette, Director points to sign
designating new site for the University of
Alberta, Calgary Branch. UC 85.025.1.24.1.

the day that the sod was turned, as I remember was a nice crisp...day, lots of sun, cool wind blowing. And it was, I think, a very colorful event because people were there in their academic gowns and all the right kind of speeches were made....[28]

The speeches were from several of the representatives of the provincial government, the University of Alberta, and its representatives at Calgary (UAC). Fred Colborne, the Minister of Public Works, turned the sod with the ceremonial spade, and photos were taken with Andy Doucette pointing to the sign designating the new site. The ceremony also included the first convocation for the University of Alberta in Calgary. Colborne declared, "Calgary is to become in every sense a university city," while Walter Johns, Vice-President of the University of Alberta predicted, "Here, in these wind-swept hills, we'll see a dream become a reality."[29] For the several hundred who attended the convocation ceremony, or the smaller group of seventy-five or so who went to the sod-turning, the day was an affirmation of progress. Indeed, the students named their 1959 yearbook *Progrediamur* – "Let us go forward".[30]

The Department of Public Works began clearing the site in the spring of 1960, creating a veritable dust storm that drifted across the road into Capitol Hill. In response to the complaints, someone in the construction crews of Burns and Dutton suggested that straw mixed with sand would stabilize the soil. However, the end result was that now both straw and sand were added to the dust, further angering the residents who received the flying debris in and on their property. Non-residents joked that "you could have a quarter acre pretty cheaply if you could catch

SAIT Campus, 1958. Engineering and Arts and Science building. UC 85.025.01.22

Construction site preparation, 1959. UC 85.025.01.03

it blowing past."[31] Peter Krueger, who had just joined the Department of Chemistry, recollects the construction site:

> I myself remember driving to this campus in the summer of 1960 just to see how the buildings were doing, and having the experience of being caught in what was the dust equivalent of a white-out – a black-out. It was a dust storm so bad that you had to turn your lights on. And then perhaps stop because you couldn't see where you were going. And then when you arrived you found you had no brakes because of all the sand in the brake drums. It was quite an experience.[32]

The two buildings, surprisingly, came in on time, and were ready for fall classes in September of 1960 despite their late start in the spring. Their functional low-profile appearance, dubbed Public Works Architecture, drew instant and unflattering comparisons to Kleenex boxes, mattress factories, condom factories, a penitentiary, and artillery sheds, among other equally disparaging descriptions. Indeed, the General Faculty Council, on January 20, 1966, resolved: "That it be recorded that this Council is disquieted about the poor design of some of the Buildings on the campus, and also … the planning of the campus as a whole…" Yet the buildings certainly were spacious in their accommodation of the entire faculty and support staff, laboratories, library, lecture theatres, administrative offices, and cafeteria – all were under two roofs!

The campus was officially opened on October 28, 1960.[33] Already, it had seventy-five full-time teaching staff and the curriculum was rapidly expanding in Arts and Science, Education, Physical Education, and Engineering.

At the convocation in November of 1961, Chief Justice Campbell McLaurin (later the first chancellor of the university) proclaimed that the University of Alberta in Calgary, "though an infant, is a rather lusty one; with an enrolment of 1,500, it already approaches in size such older and established institutions as Dalhousie, New Brunswick and McMaster." He then argued that the University of Alberta did not have enough land available for expansion with its 150 acres, but Calgary had 350 acres plus another 200 more accessible acres and therefore UAC should be allowed to grow. He urged the hiring of a campus architect to avoid the "unfortunate lack of aesthetics" that marked the first two buildings. He also made salutary references to well-designed campuses in the Gothic Victorian style such as those of the universities of Saskatchewan, Duke, and Virginia. He concluded with a plea for "complete autonomy," noting that York had already separated from Toronto. Then, in a gesture of empire building, he suggested that the Calgary campus become "Alberta Southern University, so that it will be the pride of Lethbridge, Medicine Hat, the far flung small towns and folk on our prairie lands and ranches."[34]

Although the speech sparked more public discussion, quiet internal planning had already begun regarding the future course and design of the university. The principal, Malcolm Taylor, convened a planning conference at the Banff School of Fine Arts early in 1961,[35] which represented the first major step towards future campus and program planning by faculty representatives. In establishing the agenda, Taylor had to be careful to balance the emergent competing interests of the faculties, minding in particular the tension between Education and Arts and Science. When he heard of Ethel King-Shaw's worry that the program would become an Education "put down,"

Banff Planning Conference, 1961. University Participants assembled at the Banff School of Fine Arts. From Peter Glockner, *A Place of Ingenuity*, (Calgary: University of Calgary Press, 1994).

Planning Group, University of Calgary, 1961.
Photograph includes James B. Hyne, Chemistry,
second from left, John Heintz Philosophy, fourth
from left. Photo courtesy of John Heintz.

he called her in and asked her what her issues were. She indicated that Education should come last not first on the agenda.[36] He made the adjustment, and it worked to Education's benefit. King-Shaw was also the recording secretary, and thereby influenced both the agenda and output of the conference.

The dialogue among the participants was both philosophical and pragmatic. The faculty struggled with the balance between the sciences and the humanities, between disciplinary integrity and interdisciplinarity, between the professional aspirations of community and the academic nurture of a "community of scholars." On the practical side, the Banff Conference passed fourteen resolutions. The most crucial of these were: a common core of courses for all students; avoidance of segregation of professional and non-professional students, combined with the necessity of the professional schools within the university; the development of interdisciplinary study and research (e.g., Latin American and Indian Studies); the development of inter-departmental and inter-faculty seminars; cross-departmental and faculty hiring; and the establishment of liaison committees between departments. Integration of knowledge tending towards a unified field of knowledge informed much of the discussion and was hence reflected in the resolutions.

The fledgling university also became practised in proximate social relations in those two small and rather crowded buildings. Roland Lambert, an educational psychology professor in those days, captures the feeling of community and non-hierarchical social structure:

> We all ate in the same restaurant if you like, and all at the same cafeteria. We knew all the professors in the whole University. We knew all the students in the whole University. It was like a big family. The numbers were sufficiently small so that I could talk to a Physics member at noon for an hour if I wanted to and stuff like that. I knew every professor in the institution, including the President, who we spoke to on a first-name basis. You didn't have sixteen lawyers and administrators between the so-called professor and the big wheel president. He was just another guy. We knew him well.[37]

The same sense of social intimacy is described by Donald Mills, then a newly-hired sociologist from California.

> Because it was an emerging university, growing rather quickly, it was necessary to create a suitable academic culture. Each of us would invoke elements from our own academic experiences, and it was not uncommon to see those schooled in the British tradition wearing their black academic gown to lectures. The 'hard" scientists set themselves apart by donning an equally obvious status symbol: the white lab coat. Faculty members, whatever their discipline, would gather with support staff at 10 and 2 for coffee, when our small numbers permitted all those free from lecturing responsibilities to gather in one room of the Administration Building. Additionally, there were teas and holiday parties, and wives were expected to organize large dances in addition to entertaining at home. The significant role played by spouses in academic life in the early years cannot be emphasized too greatly...[38]

Victor Mitchell was the first member of the Department of Drama, and he notes with some irony the drama department's early struggle for identity.

> There was no office for the Department of Drama – there was no Department of Drama! So we found a piece of plywood and plopped it on top of the basin that the janitors used for cleaning their mops and we ran a long cord down the Arts Building corridor to the Music Department. I had to sit in the hallway, where I'd pinned a sign: Department of Drama.

Quentin and Joyce Doolittle arrived in Calgary with their four children in 1960. He was one of a trio of musicians to join the Art and Education Department buried in the bottom level of the large lecture theatres. Joyce Doolittle involved herself in community theatre. She bought her first membership in the Allied Arts Council when she settled in during the first year, and then joined various theatre groups such as the Mac 14, Alberta Theatre Projects, and Pumphouse Theatre. As well, she eventually became active on their boards of directors. In 1965, she was hired by Victor Mitchell as a part-time sessional instructor, and gradually acquired regular full-time status, bringing her valuable directing experience to community theatre. She soon entered the Dominion Drama Festival with the play *The Knack,* featuring Victor Mitchell's talented acting troupe, "The Prairie Players" – a cast that included Bob Haley, Sharon Pollock, and Michael Ball. The play won several provincial and national awards, though not for direction. Nevertheless, Joyce Doolittle herself did receive a dubious distinction in an Ontario newspaper: "Little Calgary housewife sweeps Drama Awards!"[39]

The social connections within the small university also fostered cross-disciplinary connections, as well as associations across age and gender barriers. Ski instruction was sometimes provided at Paskapoo (later Canada Olympic Park) by Lou Goodwin, the avuncular head of Physical Education. Others were also given expert advice: Dusan Bresky of Romance Languages gave the family of Peter Lancaster of Mathematics lessons in Confederation Park.[40] Prior to the existence of anything approaching a Faculty Club, late Friday afternoons might involve a social time at the Highlander Hotel or Andy's Circle Inn at Motel Village Inn. Cigarettes and liquor commonly accompanied engaging talk with the likes of Scotty MacNeish, Dick Forbis, Earl Guy, and George Self. Then faculty members headed out into the perpetual dust storms of April or the very cold winters of the sixties.

There were also dinner parties at faculty homes, usually given by the department heads' wives, and occasional restaurant outings, although the latter were limited by the dearth of restaurants. According to senior administrator, J.B. Hyne, there were culinary limitations to entertaining new hires in Chemistry in 1960, as one could choose either the Palliser or Hy's Steak House across from the "Peter Pan" (Robin Hood) Flour Mills on 9th Avenue, currently Gulf Canada Square.[41] In the mid-sixties, the Highlander filled some of that void by opening the Black Angus Dining Room, which served as a venue for entertaining prospective faculty appointees, visiting speakers, and other special meetings.[42] Truly, prospective hires might not have come had they seen the campus, and perhaps there was some wisdom in the custom throughout the sixties of offering positions sight unseen, by letter or telephone.[43] Gordon Nelson relates that upon his arrival in 1960, he asked for directions to the campus as he proceeded along 16th Avenue. He was told to keep heading west until he saw the cloud of dust blowing across the 1A highway.[44]

Among the active department heads doing their own hiring in the late sixties was E. Burke Inlow, the first head of Political Science. Ensconced in his fourth floor office on the south side of the Library Block, Inlow presented a formidable presence in his large swivel office chair shrouded in a blue cloud of cigar smoke in a stratus layer about five feet from the floor. A former Anglican army chaplain in the American Army, Inlow was an imposing presence with a booming voice that carried with his cigar smoke through the fourth floor where only the outside offices had walls. He hired quickly and instinctively during his tenure, with an alacrity that matched the speeding Cadillac carrying him back and forth from his home in Banff. Among his hires in 1968 was a young scholar from Duke University, Tom Flanagan, who left a strong conservative imprint on both the department and on Canadian politics. He was the first member of the so-called Calgary School, from which arose the Reform and Alliance Parties, and the regenerated Conservative Party under Flanagan's intellectual protégé, Stephen Harper.[45]

One brilliant student from Calgary was Maurice Yacowar, the founder of *The UAC Gauntlet* student newspaper in 1960. Here, he contemplates the expense of a post-secondary education at that time.

When I was moving through Central High School it was touch and go whether there'd be a university for me to go on to here. There was a small first-year and some rumours, but that was it. We had no certainty I could do a degree here. And frankly, I don't think we could have afforded for me to go to Edmonton. When I got here a second year was added, then a third. Then some of my English profs volunteered to run some extra seminars so

[we] could start our MAs here. I was not just thrilled, but relieved. Without that development here, my life would have been a whole lot different – and worse, I'm sure. Now that the U of C is so well established, I think there's a danger we might take it for granted. But I'm of the generation that frankly was saved, even launched, by this U coming along when it did … Earl Guy, Ian Adam, Don Ray – those guys gave me my career and a life I can pretty well call blessed.[46]

The *Gauntlet* experience was a wild ride for the eighteen-year-old second-year student, and he clearly decided that controversy was the way to go. He began with a scathing attack on "discriminatory, undemocratic, sectionalizing" fraternities in the second issue.[47] That was a prelude to critiques of local aldermanic candidates and campus buildings. The *piece de résistance* came with the November 11, 1960 Armistice Day editorial, "Don't Buy a Poppy for Remembrance Day," a passionate editorial against war and hypocrisy.[48] The firestorm it ignited within the community, including letters to the editor and a rebuke from the Principal Malcolm Taylor, forced an apology from the young editor, and attached a faculty advisor to the paper and its editor. Yacowar reflects, "I guess launching the *Gauntlet* when I was in second year – that remains my number one accomplishment; undiminished, maybe even heightened, by the fact that I was also the first editor to be fired. That was for good cause. It was the U's first literary issue, with a short story that seemed indiscreet at the time."[49]

The *Gauntlet* survived, and its editors carried forward with verve the lively character of the paper. The second editor, Corbet Locke, also succeeded in getting himself dismissed for a fiery editorial calling for independence from Edmonton. It infuriated Alberta's president, Walter Johns, who told him,"Young man, you're going to ruin your academic career if you continue like that." Even Principal Malcolm Taylor became frustrated with Locke, and threatened the student council, "If you don't fire that guy Locke, we'll kick him out of school." They did fire him, but not until Locke and company had put out the last issue for the year."[50]

The principle of free expression had been established, however, and future editors like John MacFarlane, David Anderson, and Kevin Peterson could continue in the spirited traditions of their editorial forbearers. As Locke put it a decade later, "Nowadays the *Gauntlet* can say pretty much what it wants. Nobody pays much attention, of course, but there's been progress in that area."[51] Like Yacowar, who returned as Dean of Fine Arts, other UAC alumni from that period came back to their alma mater as professors and administrators. Among them, were Anton Colijn, TUCFA President, and Terry White, President of the University in the nineties.

Rod Wittig, a computer science student of that era who later was involved with the Honeywell Multics supercomputer of the eighties, recollects high-spirited student antics in the sixties. He and another student, Bill Pulleyblank, now head of the research division of IBM at Watson's Lake, New York, would regularly play practical jokes on each other and on the young instructors such as Anton Colijn, filling, for example, their offices with used computer paper overnight. Norm Barnecut publicly introduced the slogan "Anton is a fink," and then had to do some explaining, since the same floor of the Library in 1964 housed the Economics Department whose head was Frank Anton, a labour and industrial relations expert for whom the epithet "fink" had real meaning.[52] Another prank involved hiding Pulleyblank in the console of the very large computer cabinet during the Open House. One of the students would tell the visiting parents to ask the computer a question, and they would receive a sonorous "ghost in the machine" response from Pulleyblank, who spoke into a large can to give an echo effect.[53]

This group did a real service to the university when the associate registrar, Julia Turner, requested help with the cumbersome and time-consuming manual registration process. Colijn, Mike Williams, and Wittig, among others, were enlisted to develop a program. It initially took twenty seconds per student to process, a time which Colijn later cut down to four seconds, and was guaranteed to avoid timetable conflicts. It held up well in registering three thousand students in the mid-sixties and was in use until the mid-eighties. At times, the ancient IBM 1620 paper tape computer with only 20,000 characters of memory had to work overnight to finish the job. As it would overheat in summer, it needed to be packed with dry ice obtained from the Chemistry Department.[54]

In 1966, faced with enrolling three thousand students who began lining up at midnight for the morning delivery of the timetables that had kept the computer running all night, the computing science staff watched with alarm from the fourth floor of the Library Block. As the students stood waiting in the rain, an unfortunate glitch developed and prevented the timetables from being delivered. The computer scientists were "thankful the students didn't know where to find them!"[55] Unluckily, the beginning of the line that then converged on the gym did see a young employee of the Registrar's Office, Gary Krivy, standing up on a table and delivering the bad news about the missing timetables. He recalls, "We almost had our first riot … I'll never forget that night." [56]

·· THE DRIVE TO AUTONOMY, 1963–66

David Brotsky and Victor Mitchell in rehearsal, July, 1971. UC 84.005.9.25.

A new $3 million library building opened on November 7, 1963, comprising five floors and 133,000 square feet of space to house 175,000 volumes, as well as academic offices in the basement and top floors.[57] Alternative classroom space for thirteen lecture rooms was available on the ground floor and also a student lounge. It was a multi-purpose structure with an attractive exterior, looking perhaps more appropriate to California than to Canada. The librarian, Dorothy Ryder, supervised the transition from the Arts Building, where she had been since first appointed in 1957.[58] The building was expected to fill gradually with collections between 1965 and 1970, and faculty and students would move into new buildings as rooms became available.

A day later, the Provincial Treasurer E.W. Hinman announced a major building program amounting to $24 million, of which over a third would be spent in the first year on the first phase of an engineering complex, student residences, expanded Science Complex, Calgary Hall (Humanities), and a food services building. In the case of Calgary Hall, Gordon Nelson, chair of the Building Committee, suggested that an arts complex would be an important addition to the community and to the university. The idea developed of a theatre in the round. It could be used for the students both in and outside the Arts faculty as a large lecture hall, as well as for public events.[59] Victor Mitchell became very busy planning a fully equipped drama facility with the capacity to present all manner of plays, despite the obstacles of diverse plans and perpetual dust.

> During those early years, people ventured outside Calgary Hall as infrequently as possible because of the black dust storms raging across campus, fed by construction holes scooped into the northwest hills' turf to construct more buildings. Students joked that there were more cranes on campus than in the Calgary Zoo. Classes were small; students hadn't heard of Drama. I was pleased to see even only three for dramatic literature. [60]

In mid-December of 1963, the details of the $12 million Science Complex were announced, notably those for a six-floor science tower by 1965, with large lecture theatres, laboratories, offices, and roof facilities for radio astronomy and cosmic ray studies. [61] To add to this positive news, the federal government announced the construction of a regional office of the Geological Survey of Canada across from the university, a decision that would, in the words of Mayor Grant MacEwan, "consolidate Calgary as the oil capital of Canada."[62]

A provincial university survey committee recommended a California model of geographically distributing faculties, moving convocation to Calgary in 1963, and creating a separate General Faculty Council in 1964. Such accommodation was favoured by some faculty at Calgary, where chemistry professor J.B. Hyne was one of the California model's more prominent exponents.[63] But no official encouragement for autonomy was proffered by Premier Ernest Manning, who pronounced autonomy

Play performed on Calgary Hall opening, 1966. Actors, Tony Nezic and Catherine Charlton. UC 82.011.02.49

"extremely premature."[64] Inter-campus relations were sometimes testy; when the president of the University of Alberta, Walter Johns, visited the campus two weeks later, he reportedly declared that autonomy for Calgary would be "useless and uncalled for." The UAC academic staff responded that this "could have only one outcome ... at each step a faithful copy of the northern institution will be produced in Calgary."[65]

Public pressure was mounting for autonomy in Calgary, Justice Campbell McLaurin once again leading the charge with claims that the University of Alberta was "mismanaged" and "lacked vision."[66] Non-academic staff grew restive as well, voting for autonomy in mid-November on the grounds of budgetary control and interference from Edmonton.[67] Faculty in Calgary seemed to chafe at the resource constraints imposed by the parent university, some complaining bitterly of Calgary's "colonial status." Students also entered the fray via the youth wings of the provincial Social Credit and Liberal parties, and the new fraternities agitated for autonomy. The activist students on campus, led by Scott Saville, wore Confederate Army caps in protest. They chanted "autonomy" outside a meeting of the Alberta Senate in the Arts Building and carried, in November of 1963, a headless mannequin wearing a sign, "Give UAC a Head". Even Malcolm Taylor got into the north-south urban rivalry, elevating it to a northern civil war, a Confederate flag presented to him by the President of the University of North Carolina draped over the podium at a speech to the University of Alberta Faculty Club. The flag was then mounted on the UAC flagpole as a visible symbol of protest. On November 23, a student plebiscite was held on the issue of autonomy and passed 561 votes to 152.

When Malcolm Taylor resigned his post as principal effective June 30, 1964 to take up the office of president of the new University of Victoria, the flag went to half-mast, and a two-ton concrete wheel labelled "Autonomy 196?" was placed by the engineering students in front of the library. Five hundred students gathered in protest in the library foyer and a telegram petition was signed by about 900 students to send to

Student protest for Autonomy for UAC. 1963. UC 82.010.01.24 5.

Taylor, who used the occasion to accelerate the movement towards self-government. He continued in his public statements to promote the idea's possible implementation in two years.

The General Faculty Council at UAC was given legal status when a provision of the University Act Amendment was passed in 1964, allowing a separate GFC, deans' council, and president for the University of Calgary. The Act of 1964 also created a Universities Coordinating Council. It made recommendations concerning affiliations, examinations, and supervision of graduate studies. In the view of Dr. Herbert Armstrong, the first president, appointed to replace Taylor, this legislation proved a first and significant step away from the California model towards full autonomy. The Board of Governors announced the two-president university in February of 1964; two parallel universes so to speak, with the GFC in Calgary the mirror image of the one in Edmonton. It was given broad powers over faculty councils, curriculum, timetables, examinations, recommendation of degrees, preparation of calendars, and hearings of student appeals, as well as the recommendation of establishment of faculties, departments, chairs, and courses. In addition, the Coordinating Council, consisting of two presidents, vice presidents and deans, and two GFC members for each, was created under an amended University Act. All of these changes still did not make for autonomy, for that could only follow upon a complete revamping of the University Act.

The formal commission to study the matter of full autonomy was chaired by Mr. Justice Hugh John Macdonald. Its recommendations in November of 1965 on new dual structures became the basis of Bill 77 and received assent on April 15, 1966 as the Universities Act. This set up an intermediary Coordinating Council and a Universities Commission as an intermediary body between the universities and the government. The Banff School of Fine Arts, under the umbrella of the University of Alberta since 1931, was now placed with the University of Calgary. As somewhat of a surprise, Alberta got a third university when the University of Lethbridge was added at the last. The formal transfer of legislative authority in university governance did not occur until the twenty-first meeting of the General Faculty Council, held on Friday, April 29, with President Armstrong presiding.

As an autonomous entity, inferior in no respect to the University of Alberta, but behind in years and much smaller, the University of Calgary was an infant institution determined to challenge its older sibling. It joined a host of younger institutions of higher learning, twelve degree-granting universities born between 1954 and 1964, to bring the Canadian total to forty-four. Calgary was unique, however, in that it had gone through an extra cycle of birth and rebirth over the fifty years or so since the death of its first college-*cum*-university. Calgary had persisted in its vision, and had generated a formidable popular will that could not be denied. Its students and faculty were now eager to take it to the next phase of its development.

Faculty Women's Club Dinner. Guests from top: Grant MacEwan and daughter Heather, President Herb and Mrs. Armstrong, Dr. Cyril and Mrs.M.Challice follow Calgary Highlander Piper William Hosie down stairway at Palliser Hotel, 1965. UC 82.010.01.62.

Final examinations in UAC gymnasium, April, 1965. UC 82.010.01.77.1

CHAPTER TWO

THE LATE SIXTIES AND SEVENTIES: GROWING PAINS AND PROTEST

The late sixties were a time of turmoil, both at home and in the larger world. Canadians, particularly those in Alberta, lived in something of a fireproof house, untouched by catastrophe but still aware of the winds of change blowing about and above them. The predominant voice of the late sixties was the Liberal minority prime minister, Lester Pearson, who effected major changes in healthcare and education, many of which had positive ramifications for post-secondary institutions in generous grants to the university sector in the late sixties, and prompted major program developments across the country.[1] These grants, combined with the Alberta government's cash from the oil and gas sector, meant that virtually anything and everything was

President Herb Armstrong and Science B. under construction, Science A and Arts in background. 1964. UC 82.010.01.46

Library and Administrative Building in January, 1967. UC82.010. 02.51 l.

29

possible. Pent-up social expectations in the early sixties gave way to an almost limitless horizon among education planners.

The same mentality of rising expectations was voiced by youth who articulated a desire for nuclear disarmament, a world without war, an end to authoritarian political systems, and alternative lifestyles, music, and food. The small voice of the radical "beat generation," amplified into the very vocal and activist "hippie," and "yippie" generation of the sixties, became steadily louder, and culminated in the sonic boom of Woodstock in 1969. It was a culture that crept gradually into Alberta. It arrived with radical professors hired from the United States disenchanted with the Vietnam War, with visiting icons of the rock music world and, finally, with visiting political radical agitators from the European left and American protest movements like the Black Panthers and the Students for a Democratic Society.

I came in as a young recruit to the History Department, one of several new members invited to join it in the winter of 1966. I received a long distance call in Ottawa from the Dean of Arts and Science, Terry Penelhum, asking me if I would have an interest in joining the University of Calgary, apparently on the basis of a single phrase from my PhD advisor, W.L. Morton, with whom I had ostensibly found "some favour." That was the extent of it – hiring was done, sight unseen, no interview, not even a phone interview required.

That's the way it was for many who were employed in the hiring boom of the sixties. Competition for doctoral candidates was fierce, and hiring was done on the spot at Learned Societies Conferences and annual disciplinary meetings across North America or by telephone, telegram, or telex. Sometimes referred to as cattle markets by prospective candidates, these provided convenient venues where deans and department heads could do multiple interviews at meetings and assess potential on the basis of a paper or even an interview in a hotel lobby or restaurant.[2] Overseas hiring required more deliberate pacing and care at times, given the great distances involved, but nonetheless international staffing was considerable during a world-wide shortage in almost every discipline. In Arts and Science alone, seventy-five new professors were hired in 1966, and similar exponential increases were recorded elsewhere in the university.[3] The new faculty of Engineering, created in 1965, saw its numbers double in the hiring year of 1966.[4] There was a similar pattern in Education, where swelling student numbers drove demand for faculty up dramatically from thirty-two in the early sixties to ninety-four a decade later.[5]

This explosive growth was due to student enrolment on the demand side and, on the supply side, a provincial government awash in oil revenues. Growth was also driven institutionally by the planning of the General Faculty Council and its standing committees, Academic Planning and Campus Planning. In fact, much of the future growth of the university was shaped by these groups in the late sixties, and brought with it attendant growing pains and strains. Almost immediately, pressures came not only to increase existing programs, but also to create entirely new ones such as Architecture, Social Welfare, Fine Arts, Medicine and Nursing. The new GFC produced resolution after resolution in its first two years, creating the future university with President Armstrong wielding his symbolic geologist's stone gavel of approval for all of them until his departure in 1968.

The creation of the Masters in Social Work was one such program. Its creation dated back to a determination of the University of Alberta to support a School of Social Work degree in Calgary. In the end, it was granted as a graduate degree program in December of 1966 in exchange for Library Sciences going to Edmonton. Shortly thereafter, in the spring of 1967, GFC gave approval for a new Faculty of Fine Arts, detaching it from the previously existing Department of Fine Arts and Art Education. It was proposed as a union of the faculties of Art, Music, and Drama under one roof, and it was the first of its kind in Canada. The vote, however, was quite narrow, owing to the concerns of Education, which lost a number of courses, and of others about such an untried experiment.[6]

Yet another creation of GFC late in 1966 was a new faculty of Commerce. After some debate about its name over the next year, it was decided to call it the Faculty of Business, so as not to impede its potential with a "school" designation such as that of Social Work and Physical Education.[7] The implementation of faculty status passed narrowly, by one vote, on May 11, 1967. A new dean, Dr. James Robinson, a Canadian working for the American Assembly of Collegiate Schools of Business, soon took up his duties – without staff or space, and with very little budget to mount classes in September. Fortunately, he was able to tap into the supportive business community to find part-time instructors on short notice.[8]

The health sciences were yet another area of potential expansion earmarked for growth by the first-year General Faculty Council. The Calgary University Committee had in 1955 recommended that the CUC seriously consider coordinating with the proposed new hospital (Foothills) by providing a new medical school and nurses' training school.[9] In 1964, Principal Malcolm Taylor reported that the Foothills had plans to establish a new medical school with or without consulting the University of Alberta.[10] He recommended that UAC "immediately act to affiliate with the Hospital" to ensure the university's interest. This led, eventually, to the Board approval of a medical school in principle on November 1, 1965. Early in 1966, Taylor's successor President Armstrong declared to the Canadian Association of Medical Clinicians that a medical school in Calgary would be able to produce "top-notch" graduates.[11]

The Foothills School of Nursing successfully negotiated a program that would be subject to the General Faculty Council of UAC. Nursing students were required to take sociology and psychology courses at the university in their first year.[12] In addition, they would have access to the library and the student union and their diplomas signed by the university registrar.[13] At the same time, the Alberta Association of Registered Nurses (AARN) was negotiating with the university's Academic Planning Committee about setting up a degree program and integrating it with the Foothills Hospital program; the details were to be worked out by the Vice-President Academic, Walter Trost. By 1968, a university baccalaureate was recommended for acceptance to GFC. It was accepted, but not before some tangential discussion of the proper type of skirts to be worn by nurses registered in the newly affiliated program.[14]

Fred Terentiuk, a member of the Academic Planning Committee, was recruited for extra duty by the President to act as dean of the new School of Nursing. With the school in transition from second to third years, and a fourth yet to come, Terentiuk found that "what was supposed to be a two-month deal turned into twenty-two months, and I had the honour, and I do to this day feel it was a significant honour, of graduating the first class of nursing students from this university." The students, he also noted, were "guinea pigs to some extent, but they were expected to play a leadership role … for the students who were coming in. They deserve a lot of accolades. In fact, I have to think one of my proudest moments was when that class graduated."[15]

The medical school began with the appointment of W.A. "Bill" Cochrane as the first dean of medicine.[16] Cochrane first concentrated on establishing a distinctive curriculum and philosophy of medical education that emphasized student responsibility and regular evaluation, as well as holding interviews with incoming students to determine their adaptability to this new program. Rather than emphasize a restrictive premed program, the school decided that intake would be based on a three-year general science program leading to a B.Sc. Then the student would take a three-year medical degree of eleven months a year, leading to the M.D., and a further two years could be spent in general practice or some specialization leading to a PhD. [17]

Dean Cochrane needed to know, however, if the provincial government was going to provide the funding for a second medical school in the province, and to this end, he arranged a visit with Premier Manning. He asked about establishing a distinctive medical school, and was assured that while difference was desirable, if parts could be applied from elsewhere, then that was all right too. He then received a visit from the new minister of health, Jim Henderson.

He left it up to me where we might go and talk, and so I took him out to the rocks on the Bow River and Bowness Park with a case of beer, and we discussed for several hours the issue. And about two or three weeks later the Board of Governors had a letter from Mr. Henderson indicating $25 million would be available for the medical school, period. No extra, nothing beyond that. And that was, to me a very comforting outcome and a very interesting method to get the outcome to be positive. [18]

Further searches for funding at the federal level were necessary as well, given the planned cost of the new health science complex at nearly $30 million, and Cochrane hoped to tap into the federal health and welfare fund of some $500 million.[19] The medical complex planned for completion in 1970 would contain teaching facilities, a medical science and clinical research centre, an ambulatory care centre for outpatients, and a school of health professionals. All told, it was a grand vision, actualized in building from 1970–73, some $2.5 million below budget. In the meantime, the school operated out of rented space in the Foothills Hospital and elsewhere. The first class graduated in 1973, with an official opening of the Health Sciences facility held at the same time. It was, in the words of Bill Cochrane, "a very proud day for us all."[20]

CAPITAL GROWTH AND CAMPUS DEVELOPMENT

The spectacular growth cycle of the late sixties was attended by growing pains for the university's faculty and students. With such a rapid increase in student population, faculty, and support staff, and the growth of buildings on campus, there was constant disruption in the physical space occupied. Among the new buildings coming on stream in the late sixties were the Science Tower (1966), the Kananaskis Environmental Sciences facility (1967), the Physical Plant (1967), Engineering Complexes A and B (1969), the Students' Union, MacEwan Hall (1967), the Education Block (1967) and Tower (1968), and the Social Sciences building (1969).[21] Both students and faculty played musical chairs in the search for space. In the case of my own department of History, there were four moves in four years: from the fourth floor of the Library to the fourth floor of Calgary Hall to the fourteenth floor of Education and, finally, to the sixth floor of Social Sciences, as the department expanded from ten to over twenty faculty members. The story was repeated time and again in other academic

Fall Term 1964. Science (left) and Arts and
Education Buildings (right). UC 82.009.01.07.

units, which found ways and means of coping with increased course enrollees and the endless academic planning in program committees from top to bottom of the university.[22]

Construction continued unabated under the aegis of the Department of Public Works throughout the late sixties, both on and off campus. In 1968, the Deputy Minister of Public Works announced that it would only finish those works currently underway. After that, all management of further projects was to be handled by the Department of Buildings and Grounds, located in the Physical Plant Building. This meant that new construction such as the Married Student Housing, Science Theatres, residences at Kananaskis, the animal care facility at Spy Hill, and the Priddis Observatory, the Library Tower, Earth Sciences, Health Sciences, and Biological Sciences would be constructed by Campus Planning and Development, headed by the Superintendent of Buildings and Grounds, Ian Duncan.[23] By 1972, the campus had nearly 350,000 square metres of building space supplemented by 50,000 more of residence accommodation. For nearly a decade after that, there was a virtual stop in capital grants for new development, and the campus took on a stable look until the early eighties.

One unfortunate lapse occurred in January of 1968, during construction on the Education Tower. The cement contractors completely bypassed the fifth floor of the building, building five additional stairs to and from the landing and leaving the fifth accessible only by elevators not yet in service. As the beleaguered construction foreman sheepishly explained to the *Gauntlet* reporter, "We were sort of hoping that no-one else would find out about it until we had fixed it up ... I guess that you could say we really blew it."[24] The stairs had to be removed and replaced at an approximate cost of $30,000, somewhat delaying the construction schedule for the $5.3 million building. A permanent oddity was created in that the elevator system only went to the thirteenth floor of the fourteen-story building, resulting in a walk-up

Students' Union Building under Construction, August, 1967. UC 82.010. 03.15 1.

to fourteen. As a consequence, in the first year, 1968, its occupants were graduate students; in the second, the History Department was moved in on a temporary basis; and in the third, the fledgling Faculty of Nursing became its reluctant occupants, with its director, Shirley Good, lamenting that the location was a sign of the marginalization of the faculty. [25]

A ghost story also evolved around the Faculty Club, located on the seventh floor of the Earth Sciences Building in the seventies. A former student employee, Shannon Seefeldt, now an architect in Seattle, was the last employee involved in cleaning up. She recollects that she looked up and "walking towards me was a pleasant looking woman. She didn't frighten me, but I immediately wondered how she got in with the doors bolted. All of this happened within a few seconds, and before I could even get my thoughts straight, she faded in her path towards me." After her panic, and a rescue by her mother, she told the club manager the story the next day. "She didn't seem all that surprised. She told me that must have been Mrs. Fish, the ghost of the faculty club. She was apparently a professor there at one time, and was there often. Apparently, she had a favourite beer, or was seen rearranging the bottles in the coolers."[26]

A comic and apocryphal story developed during the construction of the Library Tower. According to the *Gauntlet*, the Library Tower was intended to be much higher than the current tower, since it would clearly sink because "when it came to putting in the foundations, some of the first piles that were sunk for foundations disappeared. When more were sunk to replace them, some of the original piles began to rise again. A building any higher than the current height of fourteen stories would be structurally unsafe."[27] The *Gauntlet* also claimed the top seven stories were never used because "when they were building, they hadn't accounted for the weight of the books, and if they did expand, the place would weigh down those floating foundations so much the building would slowly become one story high."[28] Other variations on the theme of the library's unstable foundations continued into the seventies, with *Gauntlet* speculation on the library's imminent demise in a rainstorm, built as it was upon soggy sand.

University Landscaping- Tree Planting Machine at Calgary Hall. May, 1969. UC 82.011 06.29 1.

Aerial Photo of Library Tower under Construction, 1972. Note square grid walkways still prevail. UC 82.009 01.09 1.

In the years after autonomy, many steps needed to be taken to improve the appearance of the grounds constantly under stress from new buildings going up and the soil being churned around them. In the mid-sixties, the campus had assumed a dreary and bleak mudflat appearance, with planks strewn about as walkways. A decision was made to plant oats to alleviate the mud and dust problem in the section between the Library Block and the new Physical Education Building.[29] There was also a tree-planting campaign. Donated mature trees removed in urban development – widening of streets and the like – were scooped up and tethered by guy wires to keep them from being blown over. They were then planted around new structures like the University Theatre and MacEwan Hall. An opportunity arose to buy one or two of these tree scoopers from the city instead of leasing them on demand. According to the university's bursar, Gerry McGinley, this decision proved to be "one of the best investments the university ever made."[30]

As the campus grew, the groundskeeper, Walter Retzer, gradually transformed the flat and rectangular patterns of the early campus to a curvilinear garden-campus, with sinuous walkways, lush lawns, and sunken rockeries and fountains. Faced with a tough assignment, Retzer had to consider the challenges. "Calgary has one of the harshest climates around. Its growing season is short – there are only sixty to ninety frost-free days. And then there's the problem of Chinooks, which are detrimental to plant life [and] there's a high alkali rate in the soil and plants die from malnutrition because they're unable to extract the necessary nutrients such as iron and magnesium."[31] First, he used aluminum sulphate to acidify the soil, refusing to import any loam from outside, as "we built our own." Next, he put down manure during the winter, using a great deal for top-dressing and thus incurring the wrath of the football players who had to practise on it later. Then came the appeal for trees in the community: "Trees wanted, University of Calgary looking for donations." He got them, as Bob Church from the Faculty of Medicine recollects:

> Walter and I got to talking one day, and he said, "I need trees." I said, "Well I can get you trees." And so we spent, I suppose, four or five days driving around and because I was raised in this area I knew all the local farmers, I knew where they were, and groves of spruce that needed to be thinned down. And I knew where there were poplars that were about to be torn out…. And I think probably somewhere in the neighbourhood of 80% of the big spruce that are on the main campus came out of three farm groves not very far from here, near Balzac and one near Langdon. The poplars, many of those came from just north of Calgary. Some of them came off my father's ranch as a matter of fact. But it was fun. It was fun. Those were the days when there was only one vision, and that was rapid growth.[32]

Retzer and his workers built a sling with the engineering department's advice, so that it would move trees weighing up to fifty tons. And finally, the waters of the Bow River were pumped up and used for cooling the buildings and the wastewater used for irrigating 120 acres of campus. The result was a transformation from a desert-like wasteland to a verdant campus, among the finest in Canada.[33]

Walter Retzer, Grounds Supervisor in action planting trees. May, 1971. UC 84.005. 08.57

An early decision by the Board of Governors at the University was to dedicate one-half of one percent of the buildings' capital budget for works of art in public spaces on campus. The art and architecture committee, chaired by the new dean of Environmental Design, decided in 1973 to conduct a competition to choose a suitable work to complement the landscaping of the natural mall and pond constructed between the Library and Administration buildings. The office of the Physical Plant then adapted winner George Norris's design to suit local conditions, and when the academic term of 1974–75 began, Norris began work on his four-and-a-half-ton, eighteen-foot aluminum creation.

Designed to be visible from all four main entrances to the central core, it was situated atop a thirteen-foot berm at the north end of the natural mall. The work dedicated on September 23, 1975 was untitled, but it became popularly known as the "Prairie Chicken", although some identified it as an Indian headdress, an unfolding rose, or a partridge tail.[34] This exterior sculpture was accompanied about the same time by the dedication of sculptor Katie Ohe's spinning "Zipper" or, as some called it, "The Chrome Pretzel", between the Science Theatres, plus several other art installations on campus placed by the Art on Campus Committee.[35]

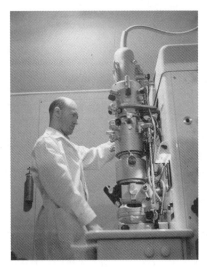

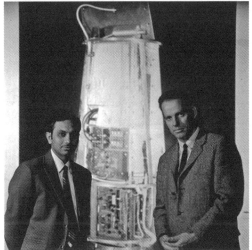

The campus in 1960 had already created a sound laboratory infrastructure in the Science A Building.[36] As well, a large talent pool accumulated as the university proceeded to hire great numbers of researchers and scholars in all fields. Early and prolific grants holders were Cyril Challice, using the recent acquisition of an electron microscope for research in the areas of Biophysics and Chemistry, and Adam Neville in Engineering, who focused on concrete research. Another dynamo was Brian Wilson of Physics, who was the powerhouse behind the Black Brant rocket project near Churchill, Manitoba for upper atmosphere research, as well as a participant in the cosmic ray laboratory work at Sulphur Mountain. Peter Krueger received the 1967 Coblentz Society Award, made annually to a scientist under the age of thirty-five whom peers judge the most valuable contributor to the field of infrared spectroscopy.[37]

Nor was there a shortage of research scholars in the humanities and social sciences. Dr. Friedel Heymann in History was a renowned Reformation scholar who left Nazi Germany after a promising career in journalism was cut short by the war. He came to Calgary in 1959, and had a distinguished career here in the sixties, publishing

Dr. C.E. Challice with Electron Microscope. Feb.1960. UC 82.010.01.12

Physics Professors Dr. Shulda and Dean Brian Wilson with Rocket, Aug.1970. UC 84.005. 06.05.

Chemistry Department, 1959. Photo courtesy Drs. David Armstrong and Peter Krueger. Top row: Drs. Frank Adam, David Armstrong, Peter Krueger. Bottow row: Shirley Bagley Swaddle (Instructor), and the department's first two doctoral students.

several books on central Europe and the Czech Reformation.[38] Heymann was joined by another distinguished scholar of German-Jewish background, U.F.J. (Frank) Eyck, whose family left Berlin in the thirties for London, where he served with British Army Intelligence in World War II. He wrote several books on German and British history. Eyck also served the university well, both on the GFC Library committee and as its representative to the Inter-University Committee for Graduate Studies in Dubrovnik during the seventies. Albin Winspear, a classicist, applied computerized methods to determine the authenticity of classical writings such as the Epistles of Plato. Most of all, he was known for his tour company's cruises of sites in the Aegean, which earned him the title "Zorba." He could be seen accompanying passengers on shore "wearing a yachting cap, smoking Papastratos cigarettes, ordering ouzo … speaking a courtly Greek to waiters. He'd sit there reading from Thucydides on the Spartan-Athenian wars with the same breeze that confounded the Corinthian fleet unraveling his white hair like loose ends of a ball of string, every inch a man involved in an important work."[39]

Yet another cosmopolitan academic to join the University staff in Economics was Stephen Peitchinis, who came via Western Ontario and the London School of Economics with an impressive array of books and monographs on labour relations, and on the Canadian wage economy. In 1968, he took on a timely study of the federal government's role in post-secondary financing that was submitted to the Council of Ministers.[40] Soon after, he was joined in the Economics Department by Holocaust survivor Jan Adam, who built a reputation as a scholarly authority on East European political economy.

A prime spokesman for the university's research agenda from the outset of the university in 1966 to 1989 was the Dean of Graduate Studies, James B. Hyne. He articulated early in 1967 some of the research initiatives, breaking them down into several categories. First, there were the externally supported research groups such as his own Sulphur Research Group of Alberta, Sulphur Research Ltd., housed in Chemistry since 1964.[41] Then there was the Petroleum Recovery Research Institute supported by the Alberta government and the oil and gas industry, housed in

Chemical Engineering. He detailed the research activities in the city/government property north of the university in the Research Park. This largely empty tract of land would become the venue for such joint ventures between city and university as the Oil and Gas Conservation Board and the Geological Survey of Canada, followed shortly by the Vocational Rehabilitation Research Institute (VRRI) involving Educational Psychology and Psychology. Added to these were such interdisciplinary graduate programs as might be approved by the Universities Commission, such as Biophysical Science, Space Research, and Linguistics.[42] To these, he added such

Residences at Kananaskis Centre, July ,1968. UC 82.011 05.29 1.

proposals as Environmental Sciences, and the Kananaskis Centre, which were already seeking government grants.[43]

A pure windfall for research in a young university fell into the lap of President Armstrong in 1965–66 while Calgary was still attached to the University of Alberta. The bequest from the Killam Estate worth some $100 million allowed four universities to benefit from the $30 million earmarked for higher education, notably in graduate scholarships, advanced research, and chairs. From the early sixties forward, the President of the University of Alberta, Walter Johns, and UAC's Malcolm Taylor and Herb Armstrong were regularly in touch over this windfall. They finally came to an agreement endorsed by the premier in late 1966 over the division of the funds. The capital sum bequest would be held by the University of Alberta. There would be three Killam Memorial Chairs, two to the U of A, and one to the U of C; the same two to one ratio would operate for endowments and salary funds for chairs. Then there was provision for Killam pre-doctoral fellowships, post-doctoral fellowships, and Senior Fellowships at each institution.[44] Calgary's representatives, both president and chancellor, had done well in the contest for the funds that proved such a great boon to research and scholarship for generations to come.

STUDENT ACTIVISM AND PROTEST

If one were able to graph the temperature and social atmosphere, it would look like a rather flat line of continuity from the early to the mid-sixties, show a sharp spike upwards in 1967, increase sharply throughout 1968–69, and taper off gradually after 1970. In 1966, students were certainly active in supporting autonomy as a local issue. This redounded to their benefit in an institution that already housed some 4,000 full-time students, a library collection of 180,000 volumes, 3,000 periodicals, and an undergraduate reading room seating over 400 students, and with 10,000 volumes.[45] A new Students' Union building was completed by 1967; two student residences were in place plus a dining centre; and more housing was in the works for married students.

In the words of Bob Dylan, "the times they [were] a-changin'." The antiwar movement gathered steam in the United States from 1966 to 1970, peaking at the Democratic National Convention in 1968, and trailing off after the Kent State shootings in 1970. In Canada, 1968 was also the high-water mark of student protest, first with the Simon Fraser strike, and then with the riots and destruction of the computer systems at Sir George Williams in Montreal a year later.

The classes of 1966 were for the most part still like many before them in the late fifties and early sixties: fairly conservative in outlook and eager to move ahead towards their chosen professions. As more than one faculty member commented, the University of Calgary was unique in that the faculty was generally more radical than the students. That would begin to change as students became more vocal and militant in their demeanor and anti-establishment in outlook. The campus radicals began to emerge, both within the students and the faculty, and conventions were challenged by an increasingly militant youth culture. We were encountering a change in style as well; men with shoulder-length hair, women with even longer straight hair, clad by the end of the decade in earth shoes and headbands.

By 1968–69, the pots of ideology were being stirred locally in response to international events. "Rudi the Red" Dutschke, a radical German student activist from Berlin, filled a smoky lounge in the new Education Tower with revolutionary atmospherics imported from the radicalized European student politics of 1968. Eager to embrace ideologies from the greater turmoil out there in the world at large, the University of Calgary Political Science Club and the Student's Union invited the Black Panthers of San Francisco to come in October of 1969. The *Gauntlet* announced their impending appearance: "If authorities permit them to cross the border, they will be speaking here October 17th in the Ballroom. The Student's Councils of Calgary and Edmonton are financing the tour for $2,000, of which $1,500 will be received by the Black Panther Party. Our progressive Student's Council can thus be lauded for financing true revolutionary activity in the United States of America."[46] The entire Black

Panther Party Platform was printed, denouncing the racist government and society of the United States, and demanding its abolition and the creation of a new political order and social contract based upon true equality. When the anticipated problems did occur, surrogates spoke to a packed and highly charged noon-hour audience in the MacEwan Hall Ballroom, with standing room only in the surrounding corridors. The entire program and the sponsors, the political science students, and the Union were denounced by education student Ed Hamel-Schey, who was greeted by catcalls like "Sieg Heil," and bombed with assorted missiles, including crutches. The speaker, Masai Hewitt, Minister of Education of the Black Panthers, gave a rambling denunciation of the American government, and announced the impending black revolution. His connection with the Canadian audience was the good work of "Mrs. Sutherland" (Shirley Douglas), daughter of Tommy Douglas (leader of the N.D.P.), in providing free breakfasts for black children in San Francisco, and being "hassled" because of it. He ended by inviting Canadians to think of forming some "Canadian Panthers up here," to a round of applause. He had made his case for radical change in America.[47] Abbie Hoffman, the "yippie" activist and one of the Chicago Seven, was also invited to speak for $2,000 at MacEwan Hall a year later.[48]

This atmosphere of activism pervaded the campus as students began to make demands of their own. If they didn't like the content or tone of a lecture, they often walked out in protest. Or conversely, if they liked the radical content of, say, a lecture on the French Revolution, they might resoundingly affirm the executions during the Reign of Terror with an approving remark for all to hear, such as "Heavvvyy, man!" The more conservatively-minded students staged sit-ins to establish longer library hours. There were also sit-ins staged before the doors of key departmental meetings to determine graduate awards, complete with attendant children and pregnant wives. These might be stonewalled, but they were sometimes greeted by a colourful retort. One redoubtable administrator snorted that he was "not about to pay for procreation," in response to demands for increased support for married students.

In some disciplines, the ideological battles generated by activists from the left were waged over the curriculum and the nature of faculty appointments. Debates over the place of Marxist theory in the curriculum were standard in the social sciences, much as the debates over deconstructionism and post-modernism gripped the humanities two decades later. Not only course content but appointments themselves became battlegrounds of a sort as academicians contested for primacy of their worldview.

Occasionally these battles went public, such as the debate over academic freedom and tenure for the popular sociology professor and community activist, Clem Blakeslee. He had, since his appointment in 1965, been an outspoken critic of Alberta's conservative society and challenged its elite with such provocative statements as, "The youthful revolution and the rise of the cities will rid the province of the cultural rubble bequeathed by fundamentalist forefathers."[49] When it came time to consider his case for tenure in 1967, Blakeslee was denied and began a two-year public battle for tenure or "appointment without definite term." This mobilized the students, divided the faculty, and generated some public support as well from listeners to his highly popular radio show. Petitions signed by four hundred Calgarians were accompanied by a rally supporting tenure held on the Eighth Avenue Mall. The students, arguably his most steadfast reporters, included the Blakeslee affair in their "mythological" version of the university's history in 1971: "And there was one a sage, Blakeslee by name, who dared brave the power of the administration and uphold the right of academic freedom. He was the victim of the scorn of some and the love of others, yet in the end he was cast from the ivory tower into the cold world." [50]

Contained in that same "Mythological History" of the university's previous decade was a reflection on the withdrawal of the Students' Union from the radical Canadian Union of Students (CUS) during the local Students' Council presidency of Luigi di Marzo, an honours student in Political Science and a Rhodes Scholar. At di Marzo's urging, the Council withdrew, but seven members resigned in protest over the issue. The rump of the old Students' Council was then displaced by another more conservative executive, armed with an alternative and moderate newspaper, *The Medium*. It temporarily displaced the *Gauntlet*, although that paper "arose again as does the phoenix from the ashes." Luigi di Marzo, in this mock epic of medieval battle, "pleased with what he had wrought, Rhode off to Oxford." [51]

Speakers' Corner, a version of the Hyde Park soapbox tradition in London, was also birthed in this time. A regular contributor to the debates was Ed Hamel-Schey, the young firebrand who had opposed the Black Panthers' appearance on campus at the invitation of the Council. Hamel-Schey would regularly appear at the Corner, drawing good crowds and berating the student audience with references to the university as a "retirement home for the pampered children of the middle class." He would launch into harangues to the gathered throng on pursuing freedom and searching for truth, "and not be[ing] slaves to the professors and administration." Always unable to resist a large audience, Hamel-Schey chose the packed house at MacEwan Hall to give a speech welcoming the Happy Hooker, Xaviera Hollander, "winning him" in the words of the *Gauntlet*, "a coveted embrace." The entire show certainly astounded Mary Nowakowski, a food services worker, who recollects, "The mob that crowded around Mac Hall that day was unbelievable. It was said the Madam drew the biggest crowd ever on campus to see her, never matched by either Joe Clark or Pierre Trudeau's visits to campus." [52]

The Students' Union in the late sixties and early seventies also espoused teaching evaluations for faculty. For a time, the Union printed and administered their own surveys, causing distress to some professors who were typecast and pilloried by their characterizations. The faculties then moved towards their own surveys, since they had largely to rely on unscientific assessment for their annual performance reviews. Thus, by 1971, the first Arts and Science Teaching Surveys were introduced by Dean Robert Wright and were developed with the assistance of the Psychology Department's experts in psychometrics. The questionnaires included questions related to instructors' communications skills, interest and impact, teacher–student interaction, feedback, and course difficulties. They also contained several student-oriented questions designed to measure their course concerns.[53]

The persistent concern for students ever since autonomy had been to achieve representation on the university's most powerful body, the General Faculties Council. The opportunity came in 1972 when President Fred Carrothers needed help from the students in combating the University of Alberta's continuing dominance. Dr. W.F.M. "Willie" Stewart, the University's Registrar and Academic Secretary, stepped down from his role as Secretary to GFC , and spoke as eloquently as he often did, this time as a simple member of the council. He appealed to both morality and expediency, in that students could provide a "living and audible conscience" for faculty members. Moreover, the university administration needed all the friends it could get:

> The government doesn't like us; the chosen servants of the government don't like us; and large, and unfortunately influential, sectors of the public don't like us either... It is a singular piece of political folly for the teaching members of the university gratuitously to antagonize yet another dangerous and powerful sector of the public, their own students. [54]

The vote carried, and President Carrothers noted that the students in the Council could now "function more effectively. They can't stand aside and lob mortars."[55]

The students entering the other-worldly spaces of academe had to learn the language of each discipline on their stairway to academic heaven, honing their intellectual and personal skills as they coped. They became interdisciplinary and subversive intelligence agents, learning the language of the new territories, sometimes inadequately, but enough to form an impression of each and find the path upwards and onwards. The ivory tower was a confounding palace of knowledge, a tower of many songs in which they learned to master and to develop their own voice.

Perhaps the most mature voice of students of that era belonged to Madam Valda, who first enrolled in 1961, graduating with her Honorary BA in 1969. She passed away in 1973 and left her estate to students, an estate which included thousands of gifts and books to be put out for sale. She had been at various times a ballet dancer at

Nice, Monte Carlo, and Paris, had taught ballet everywhere, and had even led an un-employed march in Shaunavon, Saskatchewan in the "Dirty Thirties." She moved to Calgary in 1949, and was active in the arts and service clubs, such as the Red Cross and the Calgary Chamber of Commerce. And after coming to the University in the sixties she even gave ballet lessons to the basketball team, albeit to unknown effect. Her parting advice to all students was clear: "Be in love with life!"[56]

CHAPTER THREE

EXPANSION: 1970–80

T he seventies was a decade of paradox; a backing away from
the radical protests of the late sixties, yet a progression forward with the creative impulses of democracy. This engendered
strong expressions of Canadian nationalism, not only in politics,
but also in arts and culture. It was also a decade of economic turmoil in response to the first shock of the OPEC cartel's move of
petroleum prices, from $3 a barrel to nearly $40 a barrel at the
end of the decade. Wages and prices rose in the midst of economic stagnation.

The great exception, of course, was Alberta, whose sud-
den increase in oil wealth created a surge of petroleum activity in all sectors. Great
Canadian Oil Sands, Suncor, and Syncrude moved into mega projects exploiting the
tar sands. Northern development of oil and gas projects in the Arctic surged forward,
with Cam Sproule's Panarctic and Jack Gallagher's Dome Petroleum leading the
charge. The "blue-eyed sheiks" of Alberta were regarded enviously from Ontario and
Quebec, and the National Energy Policy was born in the late seventies to control and
distribute the wealth to the rest of Canada. The symbol of the federal government's
presence in Alberta was the new Petro-Canada Building, the tallest in downtown
Calgary, locally named "Red Square." It was a focus for intense dislike of the Trudeau
government's interference in the private sector.

Prime Minister Pierre Trudeau visits campus,
MacEwan Hall, March 10, 1978. UC 84.005.21.14

The oil boom engendered an unbridled optimism in Albertans. There were 2,500 out-of-province migrants into the city each month, and combined with other immigration and natural increase, this boosted Calgary's population from 403,000 to nearly 600,000 within a decade. Urban growth in Calgary and Edmonton was the most spectacular in the nation as a whole, and continued to dominate population growth on the prairies.[1] The city spilled out in every direction, giving Calgary, at over 200 square miles, one of the largest urban footprints in the country. It was an urban planner's paradise, both in the inner core and beyond. The plus-15 concept of connecting downtown buildings became a way of maintaining the vitality of the city's centre. Other major civic, provincial, and private initiatives resulted in a whole series of cultural centres like the Glenbow Museum and Convention Center, Planetarium, and the Theatre and Arts Centres, as well as the beginnings of a light-rail system by the early eighties. Until the boom broke in 1981, there were regularly fifteen to twenty building cranes gracing the changing skyline of the city.[2]

ENVIRONMENTAL STUDIES AND CANADIAN STUDIES

As the city was in the process of being made and remade, the University of Calgary was proceeding with the completion of the first phase of building. It seemed natural to press forward at this time with one of its early plans after autonomy for a school of architecture – a plan sidetracked during the Armstrong years. The recruitment of J.B. Cragg as Head of Biology in 1966 was the beginning of a circuitous route to realize the Environmental Sciences Center in Kananaskis. When the incoming president, Fred Carrothers, took office in the summer of 1969, he asked Cragg to become Vice-President Academic, a post he held until 1971. One of his initiatives was to explore, along with Gordon Nelson of the Department of Geography, a focal point for "interdisciplinary studies in the broad area of resources, the environment, and planning."[3]

This led to a proposal to GFC in 1971 for a graduate program that included architecture degree studies, environmental science (Jim Cragg), and urbanism (Don Detomasi). Its first dean, Bill Perks, an engineer and planner, was attracted to Cragg's half-formed vision within the contexts of ecology and urban design, and the opportunities that existed at the university.

> It was my appreciation of U of C as an innovative, open-to-ideas, and structurally-change-minded institution. ... Also: "opportunity" (in the best British sense of the term) to model and build something unique for Canadian professional design studies. Also: I had seen Calgary as a community built on, building itself on *entrepreneurialism* and innovation, fresh thinking, etc. Where else to begin a new path to environmental design?[4]

Perks began to recruit a broad assortment of planners, biologists, and architects. The Faculty of Environmental Design initially accepted about ten students in the fall of 1971, with plans to accept fifty students in the next year.[5] The ensuing competition with the University of Alberta became intense, as Jim Cragg described in a letter to President Carrothers:

> Our attempts to establish a Faculty have been very closely followed by the University of Alberta. On a number of occasions, as Vice-President (Academic) of this University, I have had official and unofficial inquiries about our plans and, in particular, request for the date on which our Faculty would become operational. I think the GFC should be made fully aware of the discussions which took place some years ago and the pressures that are bound to arise from the University of Alberta, the [Universities] Commission, and perhaps the Government if our plans for action in Environmental Design are further delayed.[6]

In essence, the university had stolen a march on the University of Alberta, and there were even threats to sue the Universities Commission for approving the Calgary plan after a meeting in Red Deer saw the University of Alberta underrepresented because of bad weather to the north.[7] It is ironic that the environment played a significant part in Calgary's securing the interdisciplinary faculty over Edmonton's bid for a more traditional school of architecture.

Canadian Studies and Canadianization were other burning issues at universities and colleges in the early seventies. With the creation in 1972 of a commission by the Association of Universities and Colleges in Canada, this became a public debate as commissioner, T.H.B. (Tom) Symons, founding president of Trent University, travelled across Canada inquiring into the matter of Canadian courses and staffing. When he came to Calgary, for example, he wondered out loud where he was as he spoke to administrators gathered in Science Theatre 147, then called the Harvard Theatre. The implication of his quizzical comment was of course the colonial intellectual status suggested in the names of buildings and lecture theatres.

Albertans had already been sensitized to this issue in the *Moir Report on Non-Canadian Influences in Alberta's Post-Secondary Institutions* of 1971, and the results for "familiarity with Canadian literature" were very low. The University of Calgary faculty profile for Arts and Science was largely one-third Canadian and two-thirds non-Canadian, while the professional schools were either about equal or proportionally greater for Canadian faculty.[8]

The university's response was to establish a multidisciplinary committee in Arts and Science to look into the matter.[9] This gradually resulted in some greater number of Canadian courses, particularly in English, in Education, and in History over the next few years, some at University College, which expanded as it morphed into the Faculty of General Studies in 1981. Students' Council, under President Doug Mah, made a substantial donation of $120,000 towards an Endowed Chair of Canadian Studies in 1977, [10] and this, in combination with general endowment funds, resulted in the Visiting Professorships in Canadian Studies. These brought to campus such renowned scholars as Ronald Sutherland (Canadian Literature, 1978–79), Morris

Zaslow (Canadian North, 1979–80), and Wreford Watson (Canadian Studies-Edinburgh, 1980–81).[11]

The annual Western Canadian Studies Conferences held every winter from 1969 onwards were initiated by David Gagan and sponsored thereafter by the History Department. They studied interdisciplinary themes in western society, and their papers were collected in an annual journal special issue devoted to western Canada. One of the most successful and innovative conferences in terms of attendance and community participation was the 1977 conference dedicated to the study of Native Peoples in western Canada at the hundredth anniversary of Treaty Seven. Jointly organized by Donald Smith of History and Ian Getty of the Stoney Cultural Centre, this conference was a pioneering effort in the field.[12]

Native or Aboriginal studies, first called, "Indian Studies," had existed at the University of Calgary since the early seventies. Evelyn Moore (Eyman) of the Faculty of Education initiated the university's Indian Students University Program (ISUP), which enrolled forty non-matriculated students in the first year B.Ed. program in September of 1972, and later expanded to Morley and Hobbema.[13] This enterprise was initiated when Bill Thomas, a native himself and then Regional Superintendent of Education for the Department of Indian Affairs, noted the lack of Indian teachers for native schools. Housed in the Education Building, the program had a lounge called "Red Lodge" for socializing on campus, and gave the students a sense of home while pursuing their studies.[14] Such initiatives, plus the addition of courses in History on Indians in Canada by Donald Smith and similar offerings in Anthropology by Joan Ryan and James Frideres, gave a sense of context and place for native peoples in Canada. Similarly, offerings in Indian Studies were often in the Continuing Education program on an annual basis in the mid-seventies.[15]

Red Lodge for Native Students. December, 1972, Faculty of Education. UC 84.005.14.43

Drs. Clive Cardinal and Alexander Malycky, founders of The Research Centre for Canadian Ethnic Studies. May, 1972. UC 84.005.12.35.

Yet another emerging strength in the field of Canadian Studies in the 1970s was the Research Centre for Canadian Ethnic Studies, initiated in 1969 by members of the Germanic and Slavic Studies Department, Clive Cardinal and Alexander Malycky. A few monographs and special issues were published, some of them bibliographical, on the subject of ethnic studies.[16] The Centre then became, in 1974, the publisher of the national journal of the Canadian Ethnic Studies Association, entitled *Canadian Ethnic Studies/Etudes Ethniques du Canada*, under the editorship of Howard Palmer, a new appointee in Canadian History. Palmer published several excellent special issues during the seventies, and the journal became acknowledged both internationally and nationally as the flagship journal of the field of ethnic studies. It would remain at the university for the next thirty years. A further strengthening of this field occurred in the nineties with the creation of the Chair of Ethnic Studies and the appointment of the first chair holder, Madeline Kalbach.

The mandate in the 1980s was to develop courses that were "innovative, interdisciplinary and integrative."[17] Marsha Hanen, first an associate dean and then a dean, asked Beverly Rasporich, a strong advocate of the arts, to co-ordinate a new interdisciplinary course, "The Arts in Canada," which brought together three instructors from Fine Arts: Denis Salter (Drama), Alan Bell (Music), and Alice Mansell (Art). This course was highly successful with students, who had the privilege of three accomplished Canadianists reflecting together on their individual crafts as they were intertwined in the larger composite of the arts in Canada. Further offerings emphasized contributions by novelist and English professor Aritha van Herk, focusing in particular on her novel, *Restlessness*, set in the Palliser Hotel, and on Canadian cinema by George Melnyk, featured in his book on Canadian film.

A parallel set of initiatives in the Canadian Studies area was pursued by General Studies coordinator David Taras in the early eighties. Experiential learning was fostered through student exchange programs, and by involvement in Canadian issues political, social, and cultural. Eli Mandel, the Canadian poet and thinker, co-authored and edited *A Passion for Identity: A Reader in Canadian Studies* in his time as a visiting professor. After Mandel, Beverly Rasporich became co-editor with Taras, while the book went through four editions as a highly popular interdisciplinary text on Canada, both in Canada and USA. The new chief librarian, Kenneth Glazier, after first enduring the normal course of controversy over innovations in magnetized books, staff relations, and promotions,[18] began to turn to his great passion – special collections. In the space of a few short years, he managed to collect the private papers of Canadian authors, beginning in 1972 with Hugh MacLennan, James Gray, and Mordecai Richler. In 1973, he added Robert Kroetsch, Brian Moore, W.O. Mitchell, and Rudy Wiebe, and then moved further afield to garner the papers of poets such as Earle Birney and Claude Peloquin.[19] As he recorded in 1976, he was also instrumental with Michael McMordie in attracting the papers of well-known Canadian architects

Mordecai Richler deposits his author's papers to Library, June.,1974. Left to right: F.A. Campbell, Vice-President (Academic), Mordecai Richler, W. Belzberg, H. Belzberg, Ken Glazier, Chief Librarian, Pat Judge, Public Relations. UC 84.005.18.06

Brian Moore deposits his papers, November, 1975. Left to right: Hallvard Dahlie,Head, English Department, Ken Glazier, Chief Librarian, Brian Moore and Ernie Ingles,Assistant to Chief Librarian. 84.005.21.34.

Margaret Hess book and art donor to the
Library Collection. UC 84.005.25.31.

to the Canadian Architectural Archives; names like Arthur Erickson, John Parkin, and Ron Thom. He also attracted special book collections on French Canada in 1973, and later on art and Canadian history from Margaret P. Hess and David Coutts that, he noted with considerable pride, led to the creation "of a unique Canadiana collection … which has brought the Library national recognition."[20]

The Conference on the Canadian Novel held at the university in February of 1978 consisted of 250 delegates and included readings from a stunning array of Canadian literary talent, including Margaret Laurence, Eli Mandel, Brian Moore, Gabrielle Roy, Marian Engel, and almost all of the authors whose papers were on deposit in the Special Collections.[21] Glazier noted that the subsequent publicity surrounding the conference in the press and national media all indicated that "while heretofore such conferences would have been held in Toronto or the Eastern area, it was now Calgary which could host such a gathering."[22]

PRESIDENT CARROTHERS, THE FIRST BUDGET CRISIS, AND THE ACADEMIC PLAN

From 1972 until the early eighties, there was a virtual moratorium on the major buildings that had been the hallmark of the Social Credit government's largesse prior to 1970. Indeed, the university suffered its first major budget crisis after an enrolment shortfall of 6 percent in 1971–72 [23] produced a reduction of the provincial grant in 1972–73. The administration under President Fred Carrothers then had to plan for budget cuts of 10.8 percent across the institution.[24] Immediate and serious consideration was given to fiscal exigency, and preparation to dismiss tenured staff began. President Carrothers even offered the opinion that those staff members who were on defined term contracts would be safer from dismissal than tenured staff as the administration wrestled with the difficult options that it would have to exercise to balance

Trent University Library, Ron Thom, pencil
on paper, 33" x 46", 1967, Thom Collection,
Perspective, Canadian Architectural Archives

Toronto Dominion Bank Office Building,
Panda Associates, PAN64603-68, Canadian
Architectural Archives, University of Calgary

its budget. In the end, some creative solutions emerged from the administration and the GFC Budget Committee to avert the first real budget crisis encountered since autonomy. Fortunately, the university and its counterparts in the province managed to persuade the provincial government to move into a longer cycle of funding to avoid the short-term crisis management caused by temporary downturns in enrolment.[25] Still, the GFC considered the rules whereby dismissal for cause was decided, and determined that three consecutive zero assessments would suffice.

The first financial crisis of 1972–73 set in motion a cycle of long-term planning on the part of GFC and its Academic Planning Committee, its first four-year plan issued in June of 1972. It was a thoughtful document, which projected the university's growth to about 15,000–16,000 students by the end of the cycle, about double the figure of 1972. Limits to growth were pondered, with the amusing observation by Academic Secretary "Willie" Stewart that the real limit to growth was the diameter of the sewer trunk line down Crowchild Trail! But, more importantly, the Committee, the President, and GFC took the opportunity to speculate on the various rapid-growth (16,500) to no-growth (8,500) scenarios and those between, the most "reasonable of which indicated an enrolment of 12,000 by 1975-76." More important was the "mix" between faculties and the enrolment targets for each of the four years. The committee also established which of the new programs would go forward (Law), which would be postponed (Dentistry), and which were rejected (Family Life, Equestrian).

The Worth Report issued in 1972 received instant bad reviews from faculty and students alike. Its glossy production and advertisement-like style seemed to send the wrong message. Faculty members were horrified with the attack on sabbaticals, President Carrothers remarking that they were seen as "a grand tour of the world at the taxpayer's expense." And there were intimations of reconsidering tenure, shortening degree requirements, and promoting "a person-centred society" of alternative lifestyles and self-learning. The Report represented a threat to the self-development that had been proceeding since autonomy, as Worth was a former senior administrator at the University of Alberta and was now Deputy Minister of Advanced Education.

President Carrothers' installation, April, 1969. Flanked by Board Chair, L. Thorssen, and Chancellor J.C. McLaurin. UC 82.011.06.17.

President Carrothers about to duel with cream pies during Bermuda Shorts Day, April, 1973. Note, student's "cut-ff" shorts, Carrothers' " plus fours" or "Knickerbockers". UC 84.005.15.45.

Fears of branch-plant status and of being a manpower pool for Edmonton surfaced again. Many at the university appeared to agree with the History Department Head, John Owen, who opened the 1973 Western Canadian Studies Conference with the mock query, "To those visiting delegates to Alberta, who may ask, 'Who is Walter Worth?' the real question is, 'What is Walter Worth?'"

The university rejected the enrolment targets of 17,000 to 22,000 recommended by Worth, and reiterated the university's plan to expand to a maximum of 16,500 full-time students.[26] The city would lose, however, if the professional colleges were not developed, and certain students would suffer unduly.

Because of the expense of moving to Edmonton, Calgarians will find it more difficult to receive the education they may desire. This will not deter the children of the rich, but it is a real factor for most families. In the absence of a specific educational program, the Calgarian may have to choose a career which will be less rewarding for him, but which he can afford to enter. Thus the policy of manpower planning conflicts with the open-door policy and deprives the southern head of a bicephalous province of equality of educational opportunity. We cannot accept the fact that manpower needs will be met in the first instance by students at the University of Alberta, for we would be accepting the fact that over the long term a larger portion of University of Calgary students will be unemployed than University of Alberta students or will be diverted into vocations not of their choice.[27]

The Plan then proceeded to reject the Worth Report's call to lose the four-year degree program in favour of a two-year program, on the grounds that students would quickly recognize the comparative worth of an "economy class degree" with an honours or specialized four-year degree. It rejected the proposed "college clusters" on the grounds of cost, and the proposed External Advisory Councils as suitable only to technology programs, noting "that such councils can become professional pressure groups who may or may not produce results in society's best interest."[28]

Little was left of the Report after the Plan shredded Worth's negative attitudes towards sabbaticals and tenure as little more than pandering to "popular perjoration against the inhabitants of the 'ivory tower.'"[29] Finally, the Worth Commission's recommendations for dismantling the Universities Commission and Co-ordinating Council and the shifting of their functions directly into the government's Department of Advanced Education was roundly opposed. It would leave the universities vulnerable to direct interference from government, so that its representatives would "be obliged to confront a civil service serving departmental directives." Then, just in case the Commission had not read the response in full, an epilogue was attached indicating that the university did not appreciate the insulting adjectives directed at academics in general, a list of provocations attached listing ad hominems from "foolishness," "dishonesty" and "absurdity" to "mindless professionalism."[30]

A tense point had been reached between the university and government, attenuated by the budget restrictions that followed. The slow progress made with the Department of Higher Education over the Law School may have played a part in President Carrothers' decision to take up a post as Director of the Institute for Research in Public Policy in Montreal. His considerable skills as a lawyer, his great understanding of the issues of public policy, and his capacities for innovation were an ideal fit for the new post. But he certainly had the full support of the university's Board of Governors, whose chairman, Carl Nickle, expressed his real concern at losing "a most responsible man."[31] Equally, his colleagues and students expressed their regrets at his loss, given the contributions made by the president and his wife Jane to the university community and to the city of Calgary. No one knew the difficulties inherent in the President's tenure better than Carrothers himself who, when asked what he thought the most important attributes of a university president were, had replied, "The President must have the hide of a rhinoceros and an asbestos suit."[32]

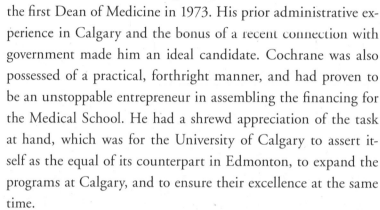
Initiation of Dr. Cochrane, Dean of Medicine, as Honorary Medicine Chief of the Stoney Tribe, by Chief Ray Baptiste of the Stoney Bearspaw Band, who bestows the honor. UC 84.005.15.03.

With Carrothers departing, the university board began to look actively for a new president, and the Board approached W. A. "Bill" Cochrane, who had departed for service as Deputy Minister of Health in the Lougheed government after his term as the first Dean of Medicine in 1973. His prior administrative experience in Calgary and the bonus of a recent connection with government made him an ideal candidate. Cochrane was also possessed of a practical, forthright manner, and had proven to be an unstoppable entrepreneur in assembling the financing for the Medical School. He had a shrewd appreciation of the task at hand, which was for the University of Calgary to assert itself as the equal of its counterpart in Edmonton, to expand the programs at Calgary, and to ensure their excellence at the same time.

As one of his first tasks in 1974, President Cochrane pushed to realize the vision of his predecessor to establish a law school at the University of Calgary.[33] Taking a page out of his own experience with Medicine, he pro-actively sought out a new dean, John McLaren, then at the University of Windsor, who had a different vision and fresh ideas of what a new law school should be. McLaren was attracted by Cochrane's experience, vision, and desire to work with people in the profession. He applauded his willingness to try out new ideas, since "we needed support for experimentation."[34] He believed that there was a necessity for interdisciplinary and cross-disciplinary work in a three-year law program in order for students to appreciate that law was part of a much larger societal picture. At the same time, he felt that there should be a legal practicum combined with classroom analysis so they would also understand better the skills that lawyers require.[35] By 1976, McLaren, who had brought with him Law Librarian Gail Starr from Windsor, had already established a library, recruited a diverse group of nine faculty members, and had run the first class of sixty students. President Cochrane then set about the reorganization of the senior administration even before his installation at the October Convocation of 1974, creating several new posts for associate vice-presidents.

Cochrane felt strongly that "an identity of excellence in the area of evaluation was important."[36] The evaluation on the first of several faculties, the Faculty of Education, was done in 1975 partly in response to community pressure from the Separate School Board,[37] and partly due to a crusading Students' Union president, David Wolf, who circulated a petition "to begin to articulate widespread dissatisfaction with the education degress [sic] system."[38]

Requests went out for submissions to the university community to be made to the Chairman, Dr. Harvey Buckmaster of the Department of Physics.[39] The five-member committee was charged to report on the objectives, academic program, financial support, organization, and management of the faculty in its report to GFC. After a year of evaluations and interviews of faculty and community, the report was made in March of 1976.[40] The Buckmaster Report, as it came to be known, was in the view of the faculty historian, Robert Stamp, "the most devastating blow ever delivered to the Faculty of Education at the University of Calgary." [41] The local press fixated on every negative detail and the recommendations excoriating "poor", "boring" and "irrelevant" teaching among other pejoratives. Even some members of the senior administration, like Finley Campbell, were appalled at the "unnecessary damage to all in the Faculty without indicating a profile of deficiency."[42] But the president was not to be deterred. The new dean, Robert Lawson, had an uphill battle to institute the necessary reforms such as the reorganization of the faculty, toughening of standards, and addressing of concerns raised in the Report. It would take four years of hard slogging by the dean and his associates.

The President established an Evaluation Research Unit in June of 1975, which would act as a resource unit to assist in the evaluation of all aspects of the teaching-learning interface.[43] Subsequent task forces were appointed to evaluate the Faculties of Fine Arts and Social Welfare (1977), Science (1978), and Management (1979). For the most part, these next evaluations were constructive in their criticisms and their public impact much less sensational than the Education Task force, partially because of the more effective input by faculties in their mandate and the careful balance of external and internal membership.[44]

The final major act of the Cochrane administration was the split of the Faculty of Arts and Science in 1976. While this was spoken of as a possibility from the inception of the university in 1966,[45] the issue did not become pressing until late in the term of the deanship of Dr. Robert Weyant, which began in 1972 and ended in 1975.[46] Weyant began to see administering the steadily expanding combined faculty, reaching 450 members, as an unmanageable task.[47] He asked Dr. Earl Guy of the English Department to compile a survey of faculty opinion as to if and how the faculty should be divided. Then the Arts and Sciences Faculty itself voted on whether or not to split, and if so, how the fragments of the whole should be configured.[48] After a 68 percent vote for a split, and 63 percent for a three-way division ,[49] the matter was sent on to GFC. It set up a Task Force under the chairmanship of Fred Terentiuk in 1975 to discuss the division, and it then began a lengthy consultation process receiving feedback from all affected departments.

Rather than adopt a more traditional split into one faculty of Arts and another of Sciences, the Task force recommended a three-way split into Humanities, Social Sciences, and Science, with a common first year to be called University College. It was an imaginative solution, although it posed some difficulties in the placement of disciplines that fell on the boundaries. Nonetheless, overall it proved workable. The University College common year gave students an opportunity to explore their options more freely, and enabled transferability from one faculty to another. Also, students were given better opportunities for common counseling in University College.

It had a provost and a college council with representatives from each department in the three new faculties, which also possessed their individual deans and councils.

An interesting offshoot of the faculty split in 1976 was the institution of an Effective Writing Qualification Test as part of the Effective Writing Program established in University College. In response to rising faculty dissatisfaction with undergraduates' writing skills, the General Faculties Council mandated the first writing test on September 11, 1976. This innovation was much to the incoming students' apprehension and, for some, extreme consternation, when they found out that they might not be allowed to graduate unless they passed the test. Even though remedial work was promised in the Effective Writing Program classes offered weekly, there was a great deal of concern expressed at the initial stages.[50] Associate Dean David Jenkins had at one point to address an angry student crowd at the entrance to the elevators on the third floor of Social Sciences, as they expressed their frustration over a needless barrier (in their view) to their undergraduate careers. A ripple effect of concern ran through the high school English teachers, who questioned the high failure rate of nearly 50 percent in the testing compared with the low failure rate of 10 percent for students in first-year English courses, and they demanded consultation in future testing.[51]

The Effective Writing Test and Program remained for at least the next few years, with some modifications to deal with the students deemed "unsatisfactory" on the test.[52]

During this period, Effective Writing Services was housed in the basement of the Education Tower, with meeting room and offices clustered in what looked like a concrete bunker. Instructors were hand-picked by Director Lebans, who "confessed himself extremely pleased with the staff he has so far recruited to teach the twenty week program." He then drummed the staff into accepting a "standard" marking code, which he and they then checked and rechecked for its reliability, so that the grading standard would be kept across the many thousands of papers marked. Under the constant vigilance of the English teachers, the students, and the deans of the faculties, he imposed a harsh regimen in order to maintain standards, achieving quite astonishing agreement rates among instructors on the codes he had imposed.

Yet another change in the features of the university by the mid-seventies was the growing power of the faculty through the University of Calgary Faculty Association, formed as an independent body at autonomy in 1966. One of its first members active even before autonomy, Harvey Buckmaster, related that its role had been important in providing input into the University Act itself. Indeed, the members would be elected by full-time faculty, rather than by rank as in the University of Alberta. The Faculty Association's role in salary negotiations grew, and as the membership grew by leaps and bounds as well, its representatives were active in negotiating improved benefits and professional expense allowances, wherever and whenever opportunities arose in the years after autonomy. Perhaps "negotiation" was not an accurate description of the process. According to Roland Lambert, who was active in it, TUCFA members presented a list, left the room, and were told later of the Board's decision. All that changed in 1973, when an arbitration procedure was established after the membership voted overwhelmingly for it in a referendum.[53] TUCFA's main salary and benefits negotiator in the mid-seventies, David Bercuson, then played with a stronger hand in the negotiations given the membership's support of collective bargaining. Coming off the salary freeze of 1974, Bercuson, as the main representative of TUCFA, hammered out with the Board's representatives a double-digit salary increase of 12 percent for faculty. The faculty association also was a parallel power in university governance in areas such as grievances, promotions policy, and benefits. Its members defined policies and procedures as the democratic twin to management and its representatives in the university administration. Negotiation and compromise almost always won the day, and if not, arbitration and carefully defined policies designed to avoid strike action did the rest.

One notable exception occurred in 1975, when one of the most difficult moments for President Cochrane came with the Alberta Union of Public Employees (AUPE) strike action in mid-winter. The local at the university decided it would try to match some recent settlements that had resulted in additional awards of ninety dollars a month; the university's administration could only find seventy. The local rejected the offer and went out on strike, causing considerable distress since the Physical Plant was operating at maximum capacity in plunging temperatures. There was high anxiety that the pipes would freeze and cause catastrophic damage, but an injunction was granted to curb the wildcat strike, and the winter session went on as scheduled without interruption.[54]

RESEARCH AND INSTITUTES IN THE SEVENTIES: ENTERPRISE UNLIMITED

In some ways, the seventies might be seen as the age of enterprise as enrolments continued upwards, ensuring a steady stream of government funding, and as oil revenues began to expand in the post-OPEC era. Anything seemed possible to the entrepreneur in the academic as well as the private sector. It was the age of Alberta enterprise; and power shifted west as government got into business, and business partnered with government.

In 1971, Jack Austin, Minister of Mines Energy and Resources, and President Carrothers met to discuss "the development of academic capacity in the energy field."[55] It was the beginning of a long dialogue between the President's Executive Committee and ministers in the Lougheed government to create in the university "an energy policy institute of an interdisciplinary nature."[56] In 1973, the provincial government agreed to go ahead with the Canadian Energy Research Institute, although the formal approval for President Cochrane's signature came after Carrothers had ended his term of office. The federal government was included and a cheque for $125,000 was received by the university on April 8, 1975, matched by the province on May 20th. The first director, John Dawson, became executive director, and soon the institute had four economists on staff, and took up offices first in Administration, and then in the Library Tower.[57]

Yet another coup for the university in the mid-seventies was the Arctic Institute of North America's departure from McGill in Montreal, where it had been since 1945, to the University of Calgary in 1975. When a committee chaired by the vice-president of Panarctic Oils explored another locale and better, more sustained funding, various competing forces came into play. First, the University of Alberta's Boreal Institute questioned having two northern institutes in the province. McGill offered free rent and a corporate donor in the shipping business prepared to solidify funding for five years. The Quebec government declared that the library was a part of Quebec's cultural heritage. They were two days too late. The injunction did not materialize until the vans with most of the library of 60,000 volumes were already across the border. They arrived in Calgary on February 3, 1976.[58]

The Arctic Institute did not initially do much better in Calgary, even though the provincial government paid its moving expenses and retired its debt to the Bank of Montreal. Typically, the government gave equal funding to the Boreal Institute in Edmonton – $160,000 annually. After some negotiations, it was agreed that the university would take over the Arctic Institute. Some latitude was given to its advisory board to raise money beyond the university grant, to run its own affairs, and to maintain the integrity of the library, with caveats against any disposal of its contents in whole or in part. It was the beginning of a long-term relationship, fraught with budgetary difficulties and private versus public perspective, but the Institute was here to stay.

Priorities shifted from sciences to the humanities. Dr. Egmont Lee of History presented a proposal in December 1975 for the creation of a research institute for scholarly research and discussion in the humanities, social sciences, and sciences. The proposal of an expanded committee from Humanities was brought forward to GFC, which gave its approval in 1976. Then the Associate Vice-President (Academic), W.R.N. Blair, took forward a scaled-down version in 1979 to the President for action. The Humanities Institute provided for Visiting Scholars, Summer Institutes, and annual Resident Fellowships.[59] Its first director, Terry Penelhum of Philosophy, was selected in the summer of 1976, and after him, Egmont Lee of History. Harold Coward of Religious Studies served as Lee's successor.[60] Building on the summer institute idea, Lee ran a conference in Rome in 1980 at the Canadian Academic Centre in Italy (CACI) established by the Canadian Federation for the Humanities, and opened up the idea of an international visiting scholarship in Rome.[61]

The research that had come to dominate the intellectual landscape of the university was apparent in the health sciences and physical education as well. The Dean of Graduate Studies, J.B. Hyne, pointed out that Calgary had positioned itself very well in the space of several years to take advantage of the research opportunities which opened up after autonomy.

> Now I am absolutely sure that the University of Calgary hadn't gone from where it was in 1960 to where it was in the late '70s when the Medical Heritage Fund came out. Ninety percent of the Heritage Fund would have gone to the U of A and not to the U of C. But it was because we had built what was clearly a university by the early '70s, so that when Bill Cochrane had taken the Medical Faculty to where it was, it was very hard for the Provincial authorities to say, you know we give a pittance to Calgary and put it all in Edmonton."[62]

In a similar sense, the Faculty of Physical Education was on its way to transformation when the outgoing President Cochrane persuaded Roger Jackson, then Director of Sport Canada, to let his name stand for Dean of Physical Education in 1978. In discussions with the Vice-President and the Committee,[63] it was apparent that there needed to be an expansion of "the research and academic profile" of the faculty to supplement the service function that it had provided so well under the Physical Education mandate of previous years. Benno Nigg, who held a joint appointment between Physical Education and the Faculty of Medicine, was well-known in the relatively new science of biomechanics – the science of the internal and mechanical

Ronald Bond, Dean of Humanities, 1966–89. UC 84 2001.037.05.01.03.

forces in the human body and their reaction. Once again, interdisciplinarity was the key aspect of his profile, since he was to teach a group of students drawn from physical education, medicine, and engineering.[64]

The increasing emphasis on research meant, quite naturally, that there would have to be an expansion in the venues for publication of research, and internal rumblings were favourable to a university press. In 1976, the Chairman of the Research Grants Committee, W.R.N. Blair, struck a sub-committee to look into a university press and to make policy recommendations. Several months later, the recommendation was that a publications board, not a press, be set up with general responsibility for publication subsidies of scholarly works and management of copyright issues. For the time being, there was a cautious approach of providing subsidies rather than press infrastructure and expertise, but it left the door open for future expansion of publication ventures.[65]

Another task force in 1980, chaired by Harold Coward, tackled the issue of Scholarly Communication and made sixty-four recommendations, one of them the establishment of a university press at a total cost of $100,000 in its first year.[66] Many of the recommendations went so far as to suggest establishing conference facilities and promotion of the new electronic technologies transforming publication. The recommendations, however, for concentration on themes of energy, law, and western Canadian studies, as well as editorial quality control, were key to inaugurating a press. Within a year, it was operational, with a staff of two and Harold Coward as Director. Its first publication was released in 1982, a study by the Canadian Energy Research Institute on alternative transportation fuels.[67]

The seventies were truly an outstanding decade for research and publication in the expansion and maturing of the university faculty. It was more and more evident that faculty members were suitable to be admitted to the Royal Society of Canada, or that they could achieve the highest honours their professions and disciplines would allow.[68] In the words of the new president, Norman Wagner, who took office on September 1, 1980, the university was in the process of becoming a world-class institution.[69]

CHAPTER FOUR

THE EIGHTIES: ON THE ROAD TO THE OLYMPICS

In 1981, falling world oil prices and high interest rates led to the collapse of the boom. The impact on the oil industry and Alberta economy was devastating, as housing and land prices broke dramatically downwards, unemployment ran up quickly from about 4 percent to 10 percent, and wages were halved in some of the trades. Bankruptcies were sharply up, and two new western banks, Canadian Commercial and Northlands, were shaken and had collapsed by 1985. Jack Gallagher's Dome Petroleum, the darling of Calgary's investors small and large, became known locally as "Doom" Petroleum after the company had to be bailed out by the federal government and the banks.[1]

Then a funny thing happened: despite, or perhaps because of, the local recession and the predictions of the demographers and planners for no growth and decline of the university student populations, university enrolment began to rise after stagnating at about 13,000–13,500 in the late seventies. Students were coming back to school after leaving for a buoyant job market in the trades, the oilfield, and downtown jobs in the corporate sector. Instead of empty classrooms, some departments and programs faced such heavy demand that lecture theatres housing 100–150 students could no longer be found on campus. Mega-sections of three to five hundred students had to be introduced in popular courses like Psychology, Sociology, and Economics to cope with majors topping 2,500 in the Social Sciences.

A lecturer had to teach in the manner of a lion-tamer or a media entertainer, in an age when multimedia productions were not yet invented. Faculty members' office hours often consisted of long lineups of students up and down the corridors, and marking loads changed the nature of instruction altogether, as multiple-choice exams and short-answer quizzes replaced term papers as the dominant course exercise. Even small-group instruction in tutorials and seminars escalated to groups of thirty and forty students, and moved from discussion to lecture and dictation. It was the beginning of a long-term trend to larger class sizes, with little or no commensurate budget increase to maintain student-instructor ratios.

Despite nominal increases in university grants – for example, 8 percent in 1979 – the picture looked different when adjusted for inflation.[2] With inflation running at 6 to 7 percent through the late seventies and 10 to 12 percent from 1979 to 1981, the impact on budget per student was negative overall in 1981, and on average adjusted for inflation a decrease of 10 percent from 1980.[3] The administration had already begun the process of considering a freeze in appointments, and would gradually move towards a policy of selective non-replacement of faculty. The ensuing debate over cutbacks and tuition increases was one that would run throughout the decade as student numbers relentlessly increased, up from 13,471 by 5,300 in 1980–88, and by almost 3,000, up to 21,575 in 1991.[4] Faced with decreases at the same time in provincial revenues and a rising provincial debt, universities and colleges foresaw a tough decade ahead.

Despite a capital freeze on new buildings for a decade, some new buildings had come on site. The Nickle Arts Museum, a result of an initial $1 million gift from oilman Sam Nickle in 1970, was completed in 1979.[5] It offered a new venue for art storage, care, restoration, and exhibition; the exhibition of an ancient coin collection; and a general venue for theatre performances, poetry readings, films, concerts, lectures, and celebrations of life.[6] For two years, it appeared that the Committee on Art for Public Spaces was dormant, but it revived in 1984 with the Civil Engineering expansion, the completion of the Reeve Theatre, and the anticipated half-percentage share of building cost from Scurfield Hall for a total of over $105,000.[7]

Like The Nickle, the fund for a Faculty of Management building was started by private donation, building on an incremental increase in base funding from the university in July of 1980. This base was supplemented in March of 1981 by a large donation from Ralph Scurfield and NuWest for $8 million with a provincial government match and a research chair from Carma Developers for $400,000. The deal was put together by President Wagner, Gordon Pearce, president of the Calgary Chamber of Commerce, and Walter Dingle, chair of the Management Advisory Committee in an attempt to boost the sagging fortunes of the faculty.[8] The unique building design met the needs of the faculty for interactive teaching and computer lab spaces, and provided a bright open atrium and agora for students to watch the electronic stock-market display and to interact with one another.[9] Tragically, the building's donor, Ralph Scurfield, died in a heli-skiing accident a few months before the opening of the building in April of 1986. A further accident, this time without injury, resulted when the suspended art sculpture installed in 1988 fell several meters to the main floor while it was being lowered to allow workers to replace lights above it.[10]

The last buildings in the eighties cycle were the Professional Faculties Building approved by the Department of Advanced Education in 1989 at cost of $41 million for a building of nearly thirty thousand square metres. In addition, another $3 million was approved for renovations entailed by vacating of other space across campus. Also added to the university space inventory were six new lecture/business theatres, two at 125-seat capacity, two at 175, and two more with seating for 400. Some of the dedicated space contained special features to suit the particular faculties moving in, notably Law, Nursing, Social Work, and Environmental Design. In addition, other support units like Printing Services, Employee Relations (Human Resources), and General Building Support would relocate there, and Food Services would occupy some space at the lower level. All in all, it was an open and airy space, linked to Craigie Hall, Administration, Education, and the Library. No more freezing walks in winter to adjacent buildings and to public transportation![11]

Students and faculty Celebrate at Opening of Scurfield Hall, April, 1986.UC 84.005.52.30.

In the meantime, eight new programs received funding in 1981 under the new program initiatives of the Alberta government. The Education Faculty received a B.Ed. in Early Childhood Education and a doctorate program in Education Curriculum and Instruction (Language Arts). Several masters programs were approved for Communications Studies, Environmental (Industrial) Design, Theatre and Music, as well as Nursing, plus a minor in Computer Engineering. The programs had a capital component ($1.6 million) and operating budget ($2.6 million) with an escalator clause to allow for inflation. Other peripheral costs for library acquisitions and support for existing programs such as Geophysics and Rehabilitation Studies increased the envelope for the university by close to another million dollars.[12] The purse strings were opened by the Advanced Education Minister, Jim Horsman, as deans made their case for newer programs yet.

Research grants generated by staff on campus rose by seventy-five contracts, drawing in some $2.7 million worth for 1981–82, and resulting in the expansion of the Research Services office in 1982.[13] Finally, there was the appointment of a new director of Academic Computing Services, Ron George, in 1981. He announced his intention to upgrade the computational capacity of the Honeywell Multics OPS/68, which after three years was unable to handle all the research and teaching needs on campus. The shape of the future, he announced, was in an integrated communications network of microcomputers (Local Area Networks), and he intended to make these networks available to faculty and students over time. It would take a decade to implement, but the technology is now, of course, everywhere.

WAGNER'S WAY – A MAN WITH A MISSION

Central to all of this activity was a leader with a vision to succeed, however difficult it was to sustain in the hard economic times that befell the province in the early eighties. In his 1982 State of the University Address, President Norman Wagner maintained that since the demand for spaces in the university was so high in a recession, the university could not afford to slacken its sense of mission. He noted the recent spurt in capital building, the computer upgrades, and the great advances in research on campus, particularly in the Medical Faculty, with the impact of the Heritage Awards. While he did announce the elimination of twenty-one positions, he noted that the reserves of the university would be depleted to ensure programs were sustained. And he did not forget to say that he would support the new deans he had recently appointed. It was a well-considered survival speech aimed to give inspiration for next upturn in fortunes.

In the next presidential address, Wagner hitched his car even more clearly to research and technology. He stated that booming enrolment could not deflect the university from its basic duty to exploit its intellectual property and to exploit technology transfer in the fastest way possible. He appointed Michael Ward of the Department of Civil Engineering to explore the ways and means of facilitating technology transfer, and to explore contract research with the research park and with the Calgary Research and Development Authority across the way from the university. The High Technology Transfer Advisory Group would advise on a number of computer-assisted learning projects, microelectronics and biotechnology, and evaluation of hardware and software needs in the university.

The university had to go down the electronic superhighway, if it was to survive. As Wagner remarked to Dean's Council during a later budget crisis, he was not about "to sit around in the dark, illuminated by candles" waiting for the provincial government to increase its grant to the university. He was acutely aware of the necessity of politics and the need for universities to unite in their common cause. Almost all of the Alberta universities' funding depended on the largesse of the Conservative government in Alberta for its basic financial support, but it also depended in part on the federal Liberal government's Established Programs Financing, which had fallen from 40 percent of university funding in 1976 to 25 percent in 1979–80. The universities had to find common cause to access these "two pockets," and so Wagner was assiduous in promoting the annual Conference of Western Canadian University Presidents (COWCUP).[14] The conference promoted the common cause, the survival and growth of western Canadian universities at the national level, and it also allowed Wagner a chance for fun, singing pop and western songs with his confraternity of presidents.

ROGER JACKSON AND THE OLYMPIC DREAM

One of the deans with a clear vision of improvement was Roger Jackson, whose skills were honed in sports competition in international rowing, a gold medal in the pairs without cox in the 1964 Olympics in Tokyo. He soon demonstrated his competitive qualities as part of the Calgary's presentation team in the Olympic bid at Baden-Baden. The team included Mayor Ralph Klein, President Norman Wagner, Frank King, CODA president Bob Niven, and several other notables from Calgary. President Wagner added Fred Terentiuk to CODA as well. He had appointed him in 1982 as the Chief University Olympic Program Coordinator to monitor further discussions involving university and community.[15]

Jackson's role on the team was to outline the university's facilities and infrastructures and to garner the African vote which, with the American, counted for thirty-four of eighty votes. The money for the expensive bid amounted to about a half-million from governments, and required another $2 million to be raised, a good portion of which came from 80,000 CODA members signed up in Calgary. The key selling points for the Calgary site were the fine residences at the U of C and the Dining Centre, both of which were self-contained and amenable to security.[16] Jackson understood both the careful preparation necessary beforehand and the pressure of the end game, as he and the teams worked fifteen hours a day, meeting IOC members both publicly and privately.

> I may have had less trouble handling it than some of the others. It was nerve-wracking from the standpoint that you never really knew where you stood. We were working hard, but the Italians and Swedes were meeting the same people, having the same conversations. Rumors would fly left and right about who was or wasn't supporting you. This was the last kick at the can and everyone had to work right through till the final whistle and that's what we did. [17]

The XV Winter Olympics were awarded to Calgary in 1988. Three main venues required work: in particular, McMahon Stadium as the venue for the opening and closing ceremonies; the Dining Centre and Residence complex, proposed as the Athletes' Village; and the speed-skating oval as an outdoor facility. These sites plus related construction would require a combined capital output of some $200 million.[18]

The proposed MacEwan Hall expansion in the fall of 1984, a joint initiative between the Students Union and the Board of Governors, added to the project.[19] The provincial government committed to $14.8 million of a total projected cost of $20.6 million. It made a further match to the university's $5.8 million raised for the joint project that would add 170,000 square feet to the original MacEwan Hall by 1987.[20] At the same time, the government announced that it would finally match the entirety of funds raised from the private sector by Alberta colleges and universities over the last four years. The entire envelope, it was hoped, would help create operating endowments of nearly $10 million annually.[21]

Further improvements to infrastructure separate from the grand Olympic plan were underway. There was yet another expansion of student residence capacity by 250 beds in another three buildings (Castle, Brewster, and Norquay Halls), which

were started in 1982 and completed in 1985.[22] On top of this, the Athletes' Village bed capacity of 2,000 beds went forward, totally funded by the Alberta government. Other upgrades to McMahon Stadium planned for the four years between 1983 and 1987 followed, at the cost of $15 million, with the addition of the Olympic Volunteer Center among the first in priority.[23]

THE EIGHTIES
DEANS

Photo courtesy of Roger Jackson. Dean Jackson aboard, braking sod for Olympic Oval.

Still other deans had a clear vision of the future and the roadmap to get there. One was Michael Maher, the new Dean of Management in 1981. Maher took charge of a faculty that had been given an indifferent report card in 1979, and determined to change that as soon as possible with a new building and new programs. He took charge of the MBA program and, possessed of boundless energy, began to overhaul the undergraduate program with his associate and assistant deans, Brent Ritchie and Vern Jones, planning the new building to fit the faculty and programs. Dean Maher was well-known in the downtown business sector, and maintained the strong sense of community fostered by his Saskatchewan upbringing. Faculty members and support staff found his small-town banter and management by walkabout an effective approach to team-building.

Deans are proud parents, usually more when they leave than when they begin. They begin by believing their faculties are worth investing in, and usually leave thinking they have made a positive difference in their development. Some deans were given programs that came and went in the eighties, such as the first cadre of new faculties derived from the original Faculty of Arts and Science, while others were at the head of a new faculty such as General Studies. Others inherited faculties troubled in the recent past, such as Education, Physical Education, and Management, and yet other deans had stepped into shoes that were hard to fill, since they were second to the original founders, as in Medicine, Law, EVDS, and Social Work. There were yet others who had continuity right from the beginning, such as the dean of Graduate Studies. Mostly, they were proud parents who would stand and deliver for their faculties.

Robert Weyant uses this metaphor of parenthood in his reminiscence, "On the Care and Feeding of an Infant Faculty." It recalls the birth and nurturing of the Faculty of General Studies.[24] Weyant relates how the interdisciplinary areas were generated in the Faculty of Arts and Science in the seventies under the listing of "Interest Areas" in the university calendar. He notes that there were already in place two interdisciplinary programs in Latin American Studies and Women's Studies in the seventies, but students were taking clusters of courses in various areas that might in the future be identified as possible programs. In the process of tracking these footprints to different courses, Weyant grouped these together and put a faculty coordinator in charge of them – a process not much different from that of Buildings and Grounds, which put university sidewalks where the students persistently walked off the grid.

Then after the split in 1976, University College became the home of interdisciplinary courses and programs under the charge of Marsha Hanen. When University College was evaluated in the late seventies, the external assessor was taken to lunch and harangued by Weyant and Hanen about the need for interdisciplinary studies to have a home. Nor did the university faculty always have a positive reaction; and at times younger colleagues were often afraid to express their support to deans and department heads for fear of repercussions. Weyant finds it "fascinating to learn recently that interdisciplinarity is now one of the cornerstones of the whole University's curriculum."[25]

The assessment committee in the end recommended that the College become a Faculty of General Studies. Weyant became Dean, and Hanen the Associate Dean in 1981; she succeeded him as Dean in 1986. Times were tough for new appointments, but Weyant had a cadre of highly qualified staff who were part of the Effective Writing Service, and who had been on year to year appointments. Approaching Vice-President Peter Krueger, "who had a sense of right and wrong," he persuaded him that these should be moved to tenure-stream appointments, and that they could serve in various interdisciplinary areas of instruction and research. Persuading the General Faculties Council to change the "areas of concentration" to "majors" might prove more difficult. But, coincidentally, Registrar Gary Krivy called with another problem. How could the Medical Faculty's request for designated "areas of concentration" differentiate these from the much looser designations of General Studies, which were more like majors? When the motion was made by the Registrar to designate the General Studies areas as majors to accommodate Medicine's areas, Weyant seconded the motion, concluding "that God is in favour of interdisciplinarity."[26]

Alan Robertson as the new Dean of Fine Arts experienced a rougher ride, even though he was a seasoned campaigner in education, drama, and Com Media. On taking office, he was required to yield three positions to the administration for redistribution to other faculties having greater need.[27] In the process of surrendering these positions, he lost an associate dean and had some difficulty with recalcitrant heads, but he did learn quickly to defend his faculty publicly. In the next year, he wrote a stinging defense in the *Gazette*, indicating that Fine Arts had been marginalized over the use of the Nickle Arts. He argued that Fine Arts had been unable to connect with public audiences effectively, since they had no control of theatre bookings or technical production, and the faculty had lost its place in a space shuffle that had promised a redesigned Calgary Hall for Fine Arts. In a compelling call to arms, he declared that "the resource that we represent is vital to Alberta and is pivotal to a national culture. If the arts and humanities are to provide that balance to a university, which is essential to offset the growth of professional faculties and technologically oriented programs, adequate resources must be provided."[28] Robertson recorded his unhappiness over the next six years as he struggled with the university's first sexual harassment case, successive cuts in operating and capital budgets, and "little understanding for the fine and performing arts."[29] At the base of it was a passion for the arts, and his refusal to accept any less than it needed to nurture its special talents. No one was prouder of his graduates personally, as he followed them passing across the stage of the Jubilee Auditorium. "As each one came up and filed across the stage, there was a special moment when our eyes met and we smiled at each other. It was not only a celebration of personal endeavour, but also a shared pride in our work as artists and performers."[30]

Among Robertson's genuine pleasures in life, along with acting in several roles while he was Dean of Fine Arts, were his motorcycle rides with the Dean of Humanities, Peter Craigie. Sometimes the third man included was John Hall of the Art Department, sometimes the Dean of Social Work, Len Richards. Robertson recalls the joy of "riding the wind with Peter" in the early eighties as part of the "Arts and Humanities Airborne Motorcycle Yeomanry," or YAMAHA spelled backwards, through Alberta, British Columbia, and Montana. He remembers Peter Craigie fondly:

> His good humour was always combined with courtesy and he had that joyous knack of making others happy, of laughing with them rather than at them ... I believe Peter enjoyed the privacy and the anonymity of motorcycling, along with the fellowship of the road and the companionship of other riders. He also appreciated simple creature comforts. At the end of a long day's ride, refreshed after a hot shower and looking forward to a good meal, he was at his ease – a good listener and great storyteller. We used to kid him about his healthy appetite (especially for doughnuts) and warmed to his wry grin as he described his need for "a good solid core of calories to keep out the cold."[31]

Before he was Dean of Humanities, Craigie had been in the new Religious Studies Department since 1974, had already been named Best Instructor in the Faculty of Arts and Science in its last year of existence, and was recipient of the Superior Teacher's Award in 1976. He served as Department Head and then took on the duties of Dean with the departure of the previous dean, John Woods, who assumed the presidency at Lethbridge. He proved to be at ease in the role, and often in the mornings in 1981 we would meet at the coffee-maker on the third floor of the Social Sciences building. Frequently he carried a doughnut in his hand, and when he did he would trade jokes with Grace Gray, the administrative secretary in Social Sciences, or they would reminisce about "auld reekie," Edinburgh, where both had been. They were truly kindred spirits, although Grace told the more risqué jokes. She and many, many others were saddened at his passing prematurely in 1985 in a motoring accident in the Rockies on the Labour Day weekend.

That tragic accident had direct consequences on campus for Vice-President Peter Krueger, who had just left his post in June to make way for Peter Craigie. That same Labour Day weekend, we met by chance in the Brentwood Barber Shop, and we stood and chatted as he was leaving. I asked him what his agenda was, and he seemed quite excited to be returning to teaching and his molecular research after nine years in the saddle as Vice-President. At that point on Saturday afternoon we heard a crack of lightning, a powerful thunderclap, and the lights went out in the mall. We said our goodbyes, and the next thing I knew, the news broke of the weekend accident. Shortly thereafter the President asked Peter Krueger to return as Acting Vice-President, and after that to resume his post for another full term, until June 30, 1990.[32] He took on the yoke of office again with the grace and the sense of duty to the university that had characterized his two previous terms.

Another dean lighting up the corridors of power in the early eighties was Tom Oliver, Dean of Science from 1978 to 1984. A pioneering faculty member in geology, he *was* the department when he became an assistant professor in 1959. He served as head through these years, taught many general and specialized courses, and was instrumental in negotiating the presence of the Geological Survey of Canada on 32nd

Avenue in 1964. That same year, he won the Medal of Merit, the highest award of the Alberta Society of Petroleum Geologists. When he became Dean of Science, he developed a reputation for fairness and sound judgment with a quiet but determined demeanour. His cheery sense of humour was disarmingly delightful, as were his limericks and spontaneous doggerel, such as this delightful take on one his favorite sports.

Ode to Myself
I think that I shall never see
A bogey lovely as a three
A bird that starts with a lovely drive
Straight down the middle – two forty five
Six iron with spin right at the pin
A three foot putt, just tap it in
Ah! Pars are made by fools like me
But only God can make a three! [33]

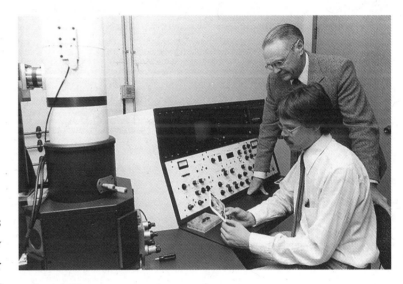

Humour and humanity can work together against the negatives imposed by budget crises and the ordinary wear and tear of daily events, as the equanimity and positive attitude that Tom Oliver brought to the office, the lecture hall, and his fieldwork every day demonstrated.

Dean Oliver instructing student on electron microscope. Petroleum Education Foundation. UC 84.005.38.36.

Deans and department heads who served through this period of grinding budgets, rising enrolments, and massive physical disruption with building on campus in the eighties needed such qualities. Dean of Engineering Tom Barton noted that the original faculty planners, Drs. Govier and Neville, had predicted that a student body of 1,200 would be there by the eighties. Unfortunately, the building complex they had proposed was never completed. The civil engineering wing just opening in 1982 was twelve years late and the Chemical Engineering building was not even started.[34] And, despite their best efforts, campus builders like Barton's fellow engineer and longtime vice-president (Services) Rod de Paiva, could not deliver engineering any more than any other faculty. As de Paiva said, "You do things as you see them and within the expectations of the time." [35]

Some Secretaries to General Faculties Council commemorate WFM Stewart's retirement. L.ro R.: Rhonda Wlliams, W.Stewart, Ian Adam, Robert Carnie, Don Black, Donovan Williams. UC 84.005.44.01.

Julia Turner's retirement as Registrar, celebrated by her predecessors, Willie Stewart on the left, Don Black to the right. September, 1984. UC 84.005.46.28.

VP Academic Peter Krueger in discussion with Gary Krivy, the successor to Julia Turner. UC 84.005.46.28.

The university lost in 1983 the services of W.F.M. "Willie" Stewart, a long-time administrator, as Vice Dean of Arts and Science, Registrar, Academic Secretary to GFC, Associate Vice-President Academic, and coordinator of the first university archives. Above all a philosopher, teacher, and orator, Stewart had panache, and exuded an aura something like the central character of the television serialization of John Mortimer's "Rumpole of the Bailey." He wrote at times with a quill pen, for he had a desk set of two with traditional inkwells and green blotter. He often peered over his reading glasses, at times with that quizzical look indicating that the question might have been illogical, and that it needed better framing. He was not fond of artifice or arrogance, and could easily prick the bubbles of the high and mighty with a deft turn of phrase. He loved the philosophy classroom above all, indicating, "In the teaching I've done over the past twenty years, I can't think of any course I've taught where I wouldn't say it had been a good class." But he did need to retire. As he said, "The pleasure of doing nothing will be so nice." And with the inevitable anecdote to drive the point home, he told of an old friend he used to visit. "He was a very distinguished fellow and he used to say… 'the old become solitary; they need their solitude as a drunkard needs his gin.'" [36]

The traditional library of books and card catalogues was on its way out, and the electronic world of the database retrieval systems was on its way in. The new chief librarian, Alan MacDonald, assumed office in 1978, and by 1979 the Vice President Academic appointed a task force to look into the potential for automation in the library.[37] The university investigated several systems, and by 1981 had identified the DOBIS/LIBIS system as the online catalogue system of choice, and the time-consuming process of conversion began.

The university appointed Dr. Stewart to coordinate archival development. The policy imperative in 1981 ruled that "destruction of university documents requires prior written approval of the appropriate university officer and the University Archivist," but it was 1983 before Jean Tener was appointed as the first professional university archivist. At the same time, Chief Librarian Alan MacDonald continued the policy of his predecessor in the acquisition of Canadian authors' papers, successfully securing those of Alice Munro in 1981,[38] and those of New Brunswick poet Alden Nowlan in 1982. The university press also began its modest operations and published its first book in 1982. Harold Coward assumed charge of its operations for the next two years, as it struggled on a limited budget. After that time, Linda Cameron was hired as full-time operations manager under the Director of Libraries and the Press. The first major publication was *The Galapagos: A Natural History Guide* in 1985, with an initial press run of 4,000.[39]

The Library continued to suffer budgetary pressures through the eighties, and major cuts of 8 percent and 6.5 percent were absorbed in 1987–89, following previous cuts and reorganization. While the book budget was exempt, and periodicals were rescued at least once by special appropriations from contingency funds, the situation was increasingly desperate.[40] The Chief Librarian noted in a public interview that some Ontario universities like the University of Ottawa had sold their libraries and that the University of Calgary had been approached with a similar lease-back deal by a leasing company. As the details were explained, MacDonald added that while selling a library may seem "the institutional equivalent of selling your daughter," there was not a danger of losing possession or control of the collection. To this Brian Tinker, VP Finance, remarked that he was not convinced "that these deals are in the long term best interest of universities, even though they appear to have some short-term benefits."[41]

The university library had by this time grown a few modest celebrities in its midst among the support staff, simply by their constant presence and their meeting the thousands of library visitors. The persons who exercise real power are the gatekeepers, and in a library these are the staff who check the library users' bags when they leave. For a time in the seventies, Goldie Nikoloff tested the honesty of the students and staff. She was of East European descent, and chattered constantly as she cheerfully sent her detainees packing down the long flight of stairs beside the up-escalator. When she died, the Librarian commissioned a folk art interpretation of Goldie in her chair at the top of the stair by Saskatchewan sculptor, Joe Fafard. Broken and restored several times, it finally found sanctuary in the Chief Librarian's office, where it sits today.[42]

Preceding Goldie, another fixture in library security was France Foo Fat, a native of Mauritius and a French speaker.[43] Librarian Ken Glazier eventually made him supervisor of security in 1977 after he had served in the stacks and three security positions – in the reading room, the main floor, and at the top of the stairs. Reflecting on the job as one where he liked "to help out in a friendly way and make them feel good when they come into the library," he notes that "in thirty-five years, I've never really had a problem."[44] In life outside the job, Foo Fat is the husband of Dulcie Foo Fat, a graduate of Fine Arts and a professional artist, the father of four daughters, and a devotee of Latin and ballroom dancing.

Another regular staff member with high visibility was Madelaine Adamson, head of Circulation Services, since it was she who determined if and whether the fines would stick for overdue books. Sometime in the late seventies or early eighties, I had been working on a book, and had taken out a book on the west coast exploration in the eighteenth century entitled *Flood Tide of Empire*, a thick well-bound hardcover. As it sat with others on the floor of my home office, its spine became a tasty glue and linen treat to our puppy, who gave it a good chew. As I returned it with the story to Madelaine, and offered recompense for a replacement, she thought for a moment and said, "No, I think I have a use for it." About six months later, as I stepped off the escalator there was a new plexiglass display case with an exhibit of the torn book and a short homily on how *not* to treat books. Fortunately, neither I nor my dog was mentioned as the perpetrator.

Chief Librarian Alan MacDonald was on a wide range of committees across campus, and even more visible in his role as University Orator, which overlapped the presidencies of Wagner and Fraser. From 1989 to 2003, he gave over a hundred introductions to recipients of honourary degrees at convocations and on special occasions. Perhaps best remembered was the thoughtful introduction of Peter Gzowski as "the cartographer of the Canadian soul" who embraced all regions of Canada from sea to sea to sea. And there were others, such as Nobel Prize winner John Polanyi , Canadian filmmaker Norman Jewison, dramatist Sharon Pollock, and architect Douglas Cardinal, all of whom received warm accolades from the university orator.[45]

University Orator Alan MacDonald, Chief Librarian, introduces Peter Gzowski for Honorary Degree. Convocation, 1989. UC. 84.005_62.19.

Environmental concerns relating to global health, issues of race, racism, multiculturalism, and issues of gender such as pay equity, the glass ceiling, and sexual harassment crossed national boundaries and made an impact on Canadian and Albertan politics. The social concerns of the sixties, which had focused on war and peace, class and power, and nuclear disarmament, had receded somewhat as these new concerns made their way into the universities and by the late eighties found many voices on campus.

One seemingly innocuous issue at first was smoking on campus and its relation to personal health. Departments and faculties were forced to abide by the official policy that the university was declared a non-smoking area, with smoking permitted only in designated spaces. This policy was a reversal of the prior rule, which allowed smoking except where it was prohibited. As of May 1, 1988, over twenty such spaces were designated as smoking spaces.[46] It was a major success in the "butt out" campaign of a rising generation of non-smokers. Exchanges at the department level became somewhat acrimonious, since smokers were identified as health risks not only to themselves, but also to everyone else. The beginning of a trend towards outdoor smoking began as the lounges slowly shrank in number into the nineties. It was a far cry from the day in the early seventies when the History Department witnessed one of its members who could not tolerate smoke request that another member cease and desist, only to be told bluntly, "I will not. No." More typical now was the vanishing smoker trying to invoke his or her license to indulge as a vestigial right. He or she was often to be told that the behaviour showed a lack of the most basic knowledge of science, and also human decency towards others.

More and more common were the smokers standing outside the Social Sciences building, braving the elements in pursuing their habit. By March of 1988, the message was that those smoking outside designated areas would be fined a maximum of $500 or sixty days in jail, although the administration indicated that it had "no intention of prosecuting individuals who ignored the non-smoking regulations effective May 1, 1988."[47] Sociologist Robert Stebbins predicted that with the declining rate of smokers from 70 percent in the 1950s to 30 percent in the late eighties, a further decline to 10 percent might be in order for 2000. But he didn't agree that the last holdouts would be treated as drug addicts, as predicted by the Addiction Research Foundation of Ontario.[48]

The other major trend of the late eighties was the move towards employment equity. There was a rising trend of women on faculty achieving the senior ranks and securing senior administrative appointments. Margaret Hughes became the first Dean of Law in 1984, marking the first in a succession of women who followed her, namely Constance Hunt and Sheila Martin, who served into the nineties.[49] Then in 1986, in the old Arts and Sciences core, Marsha Hanen, became the first woman to serve as Dean of General Studies, after spending two terms as Associate Dean of University College and General Studies. She went on to become President of the University of Winnipeg in 1990.[50] After several years in the Assistant Dean's office in Social Work in the eighties, Mary Valentich became Acting Dean in 1989, and later served as Advisor to the President on Women's Issues. At the senior administrative level, Lorna Cammaert was appointed as Associate Vice President (Academic) in May of 1985, a position she held for two terms into the nineties. And, after a term as Dean of Nursing in the late eighties, Joy Calkin became the first woman in western Canada to hold the position of Vice President (Academic).[51]

Attendant issues surrounding the place of women in the university were pay equity and sexual harassment. Both had been systemic issues for a long time at this and other universities in Canada. It was well recognized that outside of nursing and household science many fewer women were hired, fewer still promoted in the academic ranks, and that they were on average paid less over careers of the same duration. Equally, the problem of sexual harassment was revealed as serious by the Status of Women Committee on campus, which found that 78 of 286 questionnaires returned to them indicated that women had experienced "sexually inappropriate behaviour at

Marsha Hanen, Dean, General Studies (1986-90),, and President, University of Winnipeg,.(1989-99.) UC 84.005.51.28.

the University of Calgary."[52] The problems were identified by Robert Weyant, Dean of General Studies, in a thoughtful essay presented to the Senate of the University of Calgary, in which he indicated that sexual harassment was but the tip of a larger problem:

> The ethical problems here are … more subtle than those of sexual harassment or unequal pay or blatant discrimination … I see them largely in terms of unfairness, particularly the unfairness of males, who feel uneasy with women, who have difficulty dealing with them as competent professional colleagues, who turn their own problems into the problems of women who must bear the brunt of their unease and condescension. It is unfair, it is wasteful, it is painful to experience and to observe, and it is unethical. It is also time for male academics and administrators to speak out, since I have watched a number of male colleagues roll their eyes, mutter "here we go again," and tune out whenever a female academic raises the issue.[53]

The university did set about to provide remedy in the most obvious areas of discrimination with the establishment of a sub-committee of GFC to investigate the pay inequities to faculty women and support staff, and to provide redress where necessary. In the same spirit, there was a commitment to the Federal Contractors Program for equity in employment practices in all business done with the federal government. The university's performance was assessed three years later and it showed that the university's work force was made up of 50 percent women and 50 percent men, 1 percent aboriginal persons, 3 per cent persons with self-declared disabilities, and 10 percent persons of visible minorities.[54] While no quotas were set for under-represented groups, there was a determination to set targets for increase of these groups and to broaden the pool of applicants. Almost every faculty showed improvement, and pushed the university average of female new faculty hires at the assistant professor level up, so that it stood at roughly 20 percent by the early nineties.

There was an observable and parallel rise in multicultural consciousness and sensitivity to racism and human rights questions. The 1991 Canada census bore witness to the rapid rise in ethnic minorities nationally, in Alberta, and in Calgary. The Alberta Human Rights Commission heard more cases regarding employment discrimination, and the university, too, had to consider its admissions policies in the light of a new and more diverse social order. Fortunately the new Registrar in 1984 was Dr. Gary Krivy, who had been a longstanding Associate Registrar and had specialized in human rights issues for his doctorate.[55] Dr. Matthew Zachariah in Education, who received the 1989 Alberta Human Rights Award presented annually to an Albertan who "has demonstrated leadership and achievement in promoting human rights in Alberta and elsewhere," when interviewed on the subject, felt that there were four problem areas for visible minorities: work opportunities, language instruction, recognition of previous education and experience, and support in becoming part of mainstream Alberta, "instead of being given 'nickels and dimes' to maintain their heritage." [56]

Various other champions of ethnicity, multiculturalism, and diversity appeared during the eighties, notably Howard Palmer of History, who emerged as a leading national scholar in the area of intolerance through his book *Patterns of Prejudice*. James Frideres and Rick Ponting of Sociology wrote extensively on native peoples in Canada, as did Donald Smith on native history, John Friesen of Education on native education, and Diane Pask and Kathleen Mahoney of Law on multiculturalism and human rights. Ethnic literature and the arts were covered by Tamara Palmer Seiler and Beverly Rasporich of General Studies. The University of Calgary had the flagship national journal of *Canadian Ethnic Studies* from 1974 onwards. Nor could any other university have had a more active Native Students Centre, which began to mount a post-convocation ceremony every year, celebrating native graduates and their achievements.[57]

Indeed, the advances made in the eighties by all minority groups sparked challenges that their gains were based on reverse discrimination. The university had to wrestle with the fact that it presented thirteen awards that might be considered discriminatory under the new Charter of Rights.[58] The decision was made, after securing legal advice, that the awards that specified gender, age, and minorities would neither violate the Charter of Rights nor Alberta's Individual Rights Protection Act.

.... BUDGET WOES AND STREET PROTESTS, 1987

The university faced its worst financial crisis of the eighties in 1987 with the projected budget cuts of 3 percent descending on faculties when the budget committee could not meet the financial targets for salary increases.[59] The Faculty of Fine Arts' acting dean, Bernard Sheehan, reluctantly chose to cut the ceramics program, and soon faced 120 agitated staff and students, who demonstrated outside his office and voiced their extreme displeasure.[60] Subsequently, the president was petitioned by nine department heads in Social Sciences, followed by another six from the Humanities, demanding remedy for beleaguered teaching departments.

On February 16, 1987, the students even took to the streets for the first time in the history of the university since autonomy. More than 5000 students and staff blocked traffic on Crowchild Trail and 32nd Avenue and occupied administration offices to protest provincial funding cuts to universities. Chanting "No more cuts," and "Russell (Advanced Education Minister) Out, Education In," the Graduate Students' Association occupied the Vice-President's office in the mid-afternoon. Peter Krueger met the group of fifty or so students to discuss their grievances, indicating that when the final budget came down, "the graduate students [would] realize we did everything possible to protect graduate programs."[61] Faculty Association President George Fritz addressed the rally, however, and urged students to keep up the pressure, since they were the "grass roots" and had been manipulated. He then went on to note that the arch leading into the university cost four GATs (Graduate Assistantships in Teaching), and Olympic tickets cost twenty-four GATs. He was even joined by David

Armstrong, Dean of Science, who commended the students for opposing funding cuts.

The art students got into the act in the morning, bringing potters wheels into the University Theatre. They made pottery and smashed each piece upon completion, stating that "our work here has no future." They then erected a clay tombstone commemorating the ceramics program, and burned a life-size paper effigy of the acting dean, Bernard Sheehan. A mildly bemused Sheehan later confessed to Deans' Council that he had never been burned in effigy before, but allowed that it was better than the real thing. As for Minister Dave Russell, he was determined that the 3 percent cut would stick, but suggested that it might be improved in the future, since "public opinion is an important barometer." As for the student protests, he allowed, "I would participate too. It's part of student life."[62]

The administration did try in the following months to persuade the government to increase funding to the University of Calgary, this time on the grounds that the university grants per capita for Calgary were lower by some two thousand dollars than those to the University of Alberta. The case was presented to the provincial government by Dr. Finley Campbell, Vice President (Priorities and Planning), who had worked with these figures for years. The government's response was a one-man commission headed by Dr. Stefan Dupre, a distinguished economist from the University of Toronto and expert in public policy. While he did not think the current system unfair, and felt that the university should restrict enrolment if costs exceeded funding, he did suggest that it receive a one-time grant of three million dollars in recognition of its demonstrated research capacity.[63]

THE OLYMPICS: FEBRUARY 15–26, 1988

Olympic Oval upon Completion. Photo
courtesy of Roger Jackson.

The magnificent facilities for the Olympics were in the process of completion in the two years leading up to the Games themselves. In all, about $177 million of new buildings and renovations were underway by 1986, and various levels of government, federal and provincial plus OCO '88, were responsible for $107 million in Olympics- related projects. Perhaps the most stunning architecture belonged to the Olympic Oval, the first covered speed skating track of 400 metres in the world, at a cost of $39 million provided by the Government of Canada. Fred Terentiuk, the university coordinator, explained the covered aspect of the building as partially determined by the knowledge that the Lethbridge facility built for the Canada Games had to be torn down because of blowing dirt from the prairie winds contaminating the ice surface. He also explained the federal government's financing of both the Oval and Canada Olympic Park as a frantic attempt to establish some monuments after realizing that most buildings and facilities were already spoken for.[64] From beginning to end the Oval had to be constructed in less than two years, and still it won a construction medal in the process for W.A. Stephenson of Calgary and plaudits for the architects, Graham McCourt, also of Calgary. One could just stand in awe on the west campus and observe its giant roof beams and flying buttresses lowered into place, or watch the workers place triangular roof tiles seven deep and wonder at the size of this giant silver beetle two football fields in length. While other structures were less unique in their vision, they were nonetheless spectacular in their scope and variety: a $30 million expansion of the Physical Education complex made it a state-of-the-art facility; two new student residences housed the Athletes' Village; McMahon Stadium was upgraded to 50,000 seats, 38,000 of which would be permanent; and there were extensions to the Students' Union complex. All in all, it was constructed on time and on budget, in times when construction costs were relatively reasonable, and there were no work stoppages to interrupt the building.[65]

The Olympic Games were highly successful, both from a sports and a financial perspective. Careful planning of security avoided the debacles that had ruined earlier games, and close monitoring of performance-enhancing drugs avoided the major problems encountered in Seoul several months later at the Summer Games. Finally, the media legacy garnered from ABC a handsome profit for CODA, whereas previous games had proved a financial burden for years to come, as in the case of the Montreal Olympics of 1976. The weather in February was unusually warm, and the hills, except for Canada Olympic Park and Lake Louise, were unseasonably brown. But the performances were superb, especially in the relatively intimate spaces of the Oval, where the speed skaters put on graceful, powerful displays of the human form in action. Finally, after two weeks of non-stop competition, the closing ceremonies on February 28th brought a spectacular end to the Winter Games. The next day, classes resumed after two reading weeks – one more than the norm – and the ordinary rhythms of campus began again.

CHAPTER 5

TOWARDS AND BEYOND THE MILLENNIUM, 1990–2006

As Alberta moved from a troubled economy to an increasingly reduced deficit and debt-free treasury, the envy of all other provinces, it fell under the political spell of the former mayor of Calgary, Ralph Klein, who led the Conservative Party to victory in 1993. The universities were immediately put on notice that their budgets would be cut in order to meet targets of deficit reduction. While the program cuts were much less than those faced by the provincial civil service, they nonetheless applied pressure on the universities and colleges in the province to put their houses in order, and on a "family budget" basis where income and expenditures balanced. The university was looking at the largest budget cut since 1972; there would, in fact, be three in a row of that magnitude.

THE FRASER YEARS, 1988–96

Once again, the university was fortunate in its current leadership as it faced the crisis. President Murray Fraser came to the University of Calgary from Victoria, where he had been Vice-President (Academic) in 1988. He had honed vital skills in dealing with academic staff, support staff, and students through some lean years at Victoria, and was a highly skilled communicator with a background in family law. He was a

Installation of Murray Fraser as President, being helped into his robes by VP (Academic), Peter Krueger, and Dean of Graduate Studies, J.B. Hyne. UC 2001.037.03.01.

walkabout president, stopping at every opportunity to talk to students across campus, and meeting with support staff, whether janitors, secretaries, or dining centre workers, knowing many by name and by sight, and often known to them as "Murray." He also had a rapport with the students.

I often go out the door (of my office) when the students are changing classes and stop them and talk with them. What do we talk about? We talk about what they'd like to talk about. I usually introduce myself and ask them who they are, and what they're doing here and then I say "Tell me what's good and what needs change here? What do [you] think of your education here, and the general atmosphere at the university?[1]

The president established institutional priorities quickly with a mission statement appearing in the spring of 1989. He invited the university community to offer feedback to a flexible set of principles, about a dozen in number, which would guide the planning priorities in the rest of his term.[2] While he celebrated the excellence of the university, now numbering some 20,000 full-time equivalent students, he cautioned that "it is unrealistic to strive for leadership in all fields. We must make difficult choices about emphasis and use of resources, with special reference to the requirements of our outward-looking, internationally oriented region."[3] He presided over GFC with a "velvet hammer," and proved to be a great consensus builder among the many constituent stakeholders in both the university and the community.

As the president went into a second term in 1992, he became increasingly aware of the funding difficulties faced by the university. He had launched into the *Building on the Vision* funding campaign, which raised $37 million by the end of 1992.[4] Fraser was clear about the fact that times had changed for the university. He said, "I'm not living in some sort of dream land. I don't think we're ever going to get back – at least in the next 10 years – to where we were in the '70s and the early '80s when the money was flowing from the government and expansion was taking place at a rapid rate. Those days are over. The days of double-digit grant increases are over. We'll be fortunate if the government grant keeps up with the rate of inflation."[5] He indicated that in addition to corporate funding, and donations from the alumni and foundations, tuition would have to be raised – and fees were raised by 27 percent by the end of 1992.[6]

President Murray Fraser Opens new MacDonald's on campus. UC 2001.037_03.01.

Things got worse. After the leadership campaign and election victory of the Conservatives in 1993, the new government moved quickly to its anti-deficit initiatives. Soon the university's administrators were told to fall into line, and they indicated a "best guess" scenario of a 17 to 20 percent budget reduction over a five-year period.[7] The president's surprising response after hearing from the university over the year was to address the faculty, indicating that the senior administration would take a pay cut of 5 percent, and inviting faculty and support staff to follow suit.[8] The Faculty Association agreed by the summer of 1994 to a pay cut of 5 percent;[9] the three other employee groups, namely the Alberta Union of Public Employees (AUPE), the senior administrative staff (APSA,) and the senior administrative group (SAG) soon followed suit, all in all effecting a saving of $6.8 million from voluntary pay cuts. It was, under the circumstances, a brilliant strategy, and conformed to Fraser's law, "Don't be a part of the problem. Be a part of the solution."

Fraser was able to preside over two important university events in the latter part of his tenure. The first was the Special Convocation in honour of Mikhail Gorbachev, former president of the Soviet Union, on March 26, 1993, and the second was hosting the Learned Societies in May and June of 1994. In the first instance, Gorbachev accepted an honorary Doctor of Laws Degree during a three-day visit to the city of Calgary, attending a packed Jack Simpson Gymnasium holding 4,000 people. He accepted the degree, indicating that he saw it as the university's recognition of "the significance of the process of democratic reform that was launched in 1985." He went on to call for a revolution in the minds of men and women in the twenty-first century, and asked that they face the challenges of peace, the environment, and the disparity between North and South. To this purpose, he signed a joint agreement to establish student exchanges, research seminars, and workshops between the University of Calgary and the Gorbachev Foundation in Moscow.[10]

The major national event of importance to the university was the hosting of the Learned Societies Conferences in June of 1994, for the first time since their initial foray west to Calgary in 1968. "New/Nouvelles Altitudes," as the conference series was titled, was intended to draw some 8,000 delegates, and inject some $4.4 million into the local economy. With about ninety to ninety-five society meetings planned, the conferences introduced a high-powered scholarly and research component into the university and community during a two-week period in early summer, and its findings were often reported in the local and national media. The Olympic facilities were again put to good use as a forum for a highly effective series of meetings organized by Harry Hiller of Sociology, the Director of the Calgary proceedings.

At the twenty-fifth anniversary celebrations of the university in 1991, Murray Fraser honoured those who had led the institution in its early years.[11] Founding president Herbert Armstrong was feted at an autonomy celebration along with Grant MacEwan, former Lieutenant Governor, who was a city alderman when a ninety-nine-year lease was granted for the current campus for $1. With his characteristic good humour, MacEwan quipped, "I've thought I'd drop by to see if those annual payments are being made." Armstrong was honoured for being the first president in 1964. He said that autonomy was in his understanding of the contract: "I did further stipulate that I should not be installed until the government legislation had been passed and was appropriate to separate institutions, one of which was to bear the name The University of Calgary."[12] Armstrong also left the university with its Gaelic motto, "Mo shuile togam suas" or "I will lift up my eyes." There was a further remembrance of Armstrong's contributions to the university after his death in 1993, in the naming of the Geology and Geophysics Centre after him a year later.[13] At the same time, the first Director of the Calgary Branch, Andrew Doucette, was honoured by the naming of the Doucette Library of Teaching Resources in the Education Block.

Andrew Doucette, the first Director of the Calgary Branch honoured. Left to right: Fred Terentiuk, Violette Doucette, Andrew Doucette portrait, Murray Fraser. 1991. UC 2001.037.08.01.

The burning social issue in the university of the early nineties was, without ques-tion, "What was the status of women, both as students and as faculty?" The gains that female faculty had made in the eighties were being advanced yearly on campus with Eliane Silverman's development of the Women's Studies program in the Faculty of General Studies.[14] Women's issues in the Department of Sociology were being ex-plored by Marlene Mackie through her three books on the subject of gender relations, and similar research in women's studies were being pursued in Literature (Helen Buss, Jean Perrault), Psychology (Susan Boon), Archaeology (Jane Kelley), and Social Work (Mary Valentich), to name but a few. Susan Stone-Blackburn also won a vic-tory in receiving the first maternity leave in 1980, albeit retroactively, as the Faculty Association agreement did not arrive on time and she had to appeal to the president for approval.[15]

Women were now meeting together on campus to reflect on their collective ex-perience, past, present and future, although Sheila O'Brien of Petro-Canada still ral-lied a campus group of women: "I think … there's so much more we have to do. On good days I think we've come so far. Can we relax? Clearly, no."[16] Female students were also making inroads into more traditional male areas like science and engineer-ing, although less so in the graduate areas and in faculty percentages.[17] Yet a group of women, about one hundred in number, attended the University of Calgary Women in Science and Engineering Meeting in 1992 to discuss the *Women in the Nineties Report,* authored by U of C Advisor on Women's Issues Susan Stone-Blackburn, and its recommendations regarding sexual harassment, security, and increasing the per-centage of women on faculty.[18] The Status of Women Committee appointed by the President made 123 recommendations for change by 2000, its goal that the university prove a leader in the "transformation from a society whose policies and practices are generated from male experience and values and attributes to one that is truly gender-balanced."[19]

Change came gradually from the faculties, with about half reporting by 1992. There was positive action in several areas, as noted by the equity officer, Carol Clarke, in the area of Employment Equity. She reported that about 32 percent of appointments for teaching positions were women, the same number as the 32 percent of women with new PhDs in Canada.[20] Overall, the slowness of change in meeting numerical targets was normal in times of low turnover.

As the nineties progressed – and particularly by the late nineties – women were seen more often in administrative roles. Peggy Patterson was Associate Vice-President of Student Affairs in 1995; Mary-Ellen Tyler became Dean of Environmental Design in 1998; Beverly Rasporich was Associate Dean, then Acting Dean of General Studies (1997–98), followed by Kathleen Scherf, who became Dean in 1998; Annette Lagrange was Dean of Education in 1999, and Hermina Joldersma was Associate Dean in Humanities, then Acting Dean, before becoming Advisor to the President on Women. And into the new millennium, Patricia Hughes became Dean of Law, the third woman to do so since the inception of the faculty in the mid-seventies. The nineties also saw the first woman Director of the Humanities Institute, Jane Kelley, who had been the first department head in Social Sciences when she was Head of Archaeology from 1981 to 1986.

The reaction to *Women in the Nineties* produced mixed responses across campus. Some faculty voiced concerns that feminism was becoming "official ideology," particularly with reference to introducing "gender inclusive language" such as "humankind" as opposed to the more familiar "mankind."[21] Yet others dissected the recommendations concerning affirmative action and quotas, and the conflicting claims to primacy in the hiring of visible minority women over white women or minority white men.[22]

The administration also established the Sexual Harassment Office, with Donna Ferrara-Kerr as its first adviser. She embarked on an educational mission by giving presentations to new faculty, Deans' Council, and faculty and department heads. She even appeared on Peter Gzowski's national radio show, explaining the difference between flirtation and the activities described in the university's policy against

Lorna Cammaert, Associate Vice-President

(Academic), August, 1989. UC 2001.037.05.01.7.

"unwanted sexual solicitation or advances or other verbal or physical conduct of a sexual nature made by a person who knows or ought to know that it is coercive or unwelcome." It was a fine set of distinctions, as the discussion revealed, and it would take several cases on campus to delineate what was and what was not acceptable behaviour.[23] Behaviour modification was encouraged, for example, through Associate Vice-President Academic Lorna Cammaert arranging showings and discussion of the video "A Chilly Climate" on negative aspects of gender relations in universities. The annual memorials in honour of the fourteen women killed at L'Ecole Polytechnique in Montreal in 1989 were dramatic and effective reminders of the potential of violence against women in universities.[24] In 1999–2000, a first-prize design award was given to the Faculty of Engineering for a table honouring the fourteen slain women in Montreal. And more pragmatically, the Vice-President of Finance and Services accepted a generous gift of a half million dollars from Imperial Oil for the construction of a new child care facility for eighty children, which opened in 1993.[25]

RESEARCH AND TEACHING EXCELLENCE

In the summer of 1991, an unsolicited analysis of the university structure by a faculty member from Medicine created a stir that led to an interesting debate. Dr. Fritz Lorscheider suggested that two faculties should be downgraded to schools, and other undergraduate programs in Education, Management, Physical Education, and Social Work be discontinued; that Fine Arts be dealt off to the Alberta College of Art, and that EVDS, Nursing, and Law be deleted altogether. The reasoning? Medicine was being hurt by its association with inferior faculties. Although the report was identified as "flawed," "unworthy of comment," and "poorly researched,"[26] the President said that Lorscheider had raised some questions in the public arena as to the proportionate weightings that should be given to research, to teaching, and to service. What should be the order of preference in the university's internal priorities?

The president addressed the issues in his next press interview with the students in the fall of 1991. He stated that the university had some problems with both the new *Maclean's* survey of 1991 and with Lorscheider's data. First, he noted that the university was doing very well for a new university of only twenty-five years of age, and had grown to a mature size with a student admission rate beyond its budgetary means. As for the research critics, he noted that Science, Engineering, and Medicine had received three of six senior Killam Memorial Prizes from 1990–92 (Costerton, Biology; Dixon, Medical Biochemistry; and Dilger, Civil Engineering), and Dr. Len Bruton of Engineering had won the Manning Principal Award for innovation in Engineering.[27] As for teaching excellence, there were several awards and statistical measures of excellence, plus the donation of $700,000 by the Royal Bank to spend on innovative teaching technologies over the next five years via the university Teaching Development Office headed by Dr. Robert Schulz.[28]

In his measured response, the president may have suggested a balance between teaching and research excellence, but the larger provincial and national pressure was to press the universities in the direction of research. The introduction of the Canada Research Fellowships in the late eighties had brought young Canadian scholars with reduced teaching responsibilities into the professoriate. Similarly, the Alberta Heritage Medical Fellowships in Research had brought over thirty of these scholars into the Medical and Science faculties by the early nineties. By now the university had also been involved in fund-raising for endowed chairs in several faculties, the cost of which was escalating even with matched funds from the provincial government. The loss of the double match, and declining interest rates, had pushed the cost of these chairs to almost double what they had been a decade earlier. But that did not stop the insatiable demand for senior chairs that involved little teaching and nearly full-time devotion to research, and by 1995 there were thirty sponsored chairs at the

Len Bruton, Manning Award for Innovation in Engineering. UC 2001.037.01.07.

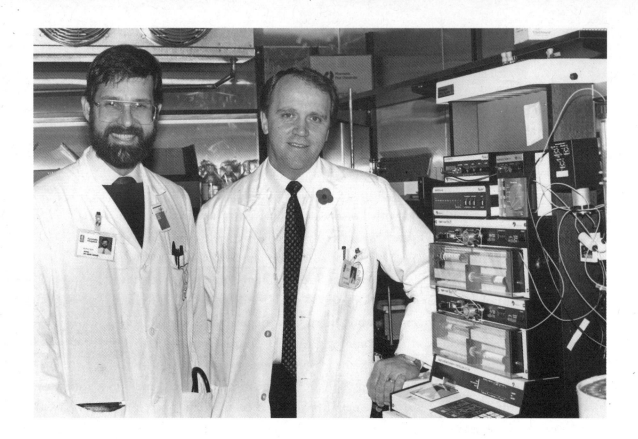

Dr. Mark Adams, Dr. Marvin Fritzler, Joint
Injury and Diseases research unity, Foothills
Hospital. June, 1990. UC2001.037.05.01.08.

university. These were followed by the Canada Research Chairs of the late nineties, a highly sought-after prize for senior professors across Canada.

Added to these initiatives were the increased opportunities to do applied research in the several research institutes on campus and in the research park, such as University Technologies Incorporated (UTI),[29] Academic Computing Technologies,[30] the Van Horne Institute,[31] the International Centre, and the Division of International Development.[32] And sometimes even small departments like Archaeology managed to pull in huge grants per capita, such as in 1992 when the department totaled nearly $700,000 for a small group of four researchers spread across the globe for their field research.[33]

The Humanities were also able to raise $1.2 million for a permanent Distinguished Writers program through a donation from Allan Markin and Jackie Flanagan.[34] Ron Bond, Dean of Humanities, noted, "This splendid gift pays tribute to the English department and its creative writing programs, and to the strong interest in writing evident in the city of Calgary." [35] The funds were a wonderful boon indeed to creative writers like Fred Wah and Aritha van Herk who had since the eighties nurtured creative writers like Peter Oliva and Roberta Rees, who was named the first writer in residence for the Markin-Flanagan program.

As for teaching excellence, there were by the nineties several awards and statistical measures of excellence, given the prevalence of faculty teaching surveys plus the Students' Union teaching surveys and awards. Good teaching was rewarded by the Faculty Promotions committees; in some faculties it was measured by formal evaluations for three decades. But the students wanted their student-initiated surveys to be the required rather than recommended means of formal evaluation. In March of 1992, the General Faculty Council passed an amendment to the Appointments, Dismissals and Promotions Procedures requiring student evaluations for all instructors, regardless of course.[36] The amendment passed after much discussion, and President Fraser

Charles Steele Essay Award in Canadian Studies awarded to Gillian Sinclair (second from left). Left to right, Apollonia Steele, from Library Special Collections, and from General Studies: Beverly Rasporich, Tamara Seiler, and Dean Michael Mcmordie. UC 2001.037.05.01.11.

David Taras Receives Second Outstanding Teacher Award from Students'Union. UC Gazette, May 4, 1992. UC 92.071.04.09.

Monika Schloder of Kinesiology receives 3M Fellowship for Teaching Excllence in Canadian Universities. 1996. UC2001.036.02.01.

Students' Union Contribution to the Library Receives Thanks. Left to right: SU President, Toby White, Library Asst. Director, Collections, Ada Marie Atkins Nechka, Director of Libraries, Frits Pannekoek, SU VPAcademic, Mark Hoekstra. UC 2001.037.10.01.

welcomed the change, calling it "a step in the right direction," because it emphasized the importance of teaching on campus.

Another development in the direction of rewarding teaching excellence was the donation of $700,000 by the Royal Bank. It was allotted to spend on innovative teaching technologies over the next five years, via the university Teaching Development Office headed by Dr. Robert Schulz.[37] Schulz continued to press for a further increase of "at least eighty per cent of teaching evaluations …based on formal student evaluations for sections with at least five students." Further success came in 1994 with the development of a teaching evaluation instrument to be administered campus-wide.[38] Other awards that promoted teaching excellence were external awards like the 3M Fellowships, ten of which were awarded annually by the Society for Teaching and Learning. The first winner on campus was Bob Schulz for his teaching and long-term involvement in coaching the University of Calgary student teams in highly successful international business-school competitions.[39] The second award went to Monika Schloder of Kinesiology, who demonstrated excellence over thirty-five years of coaching and twenty-two years of teaching, including involvement each summer in a coaching leadership program for minorities offered in Los Angeles. Besides winning two Students' Union Awards, she was actively involved in building kinesiology teams, developing writing seminars, and training peer tutors. In her forthright manner, she stated on receiving the 3M award that while she was thrilled at the national recognition, she was frustrated by the fact that teaching excellence wasn't as highly valued as research excellence is in Canada.[40]

PUTTING THE PIECES BACK TOGETHER, 1996–2001

In October of 1996, Murray Fraser announced that he would step down after eight years as president. A month later, he announced that his dazzling grey suit – *taupe*, not grey, he insisted – would be raffled off to raise money for the food bank. It was a metaphor for his generosity of time and effort to the university, since he felt attached to it, and that it was an "historical artifact ... a collector's item. It could be donated to a museum."[41] "Murr's suit sale" went on in January 1996, and a student, Sean Crawford, purchased the suit. The popular president gracefully exited in the summer of 1996, after the toughest three years, financially, in the university's history. He gave way to the next president, Terry White, with his usual grace and good humour. Recognizing that he followed in large footsteps, the new president said, "People have to realize that there's only one Murray Fraser, and I'm not Murray Fraser. I'm Terry White."[42]

White had been a high-school student at Western Canada and a student at the university before autonomy. He had also been a Dean of Arts at the University of Alberta before becoming a two-term president at Brock University in St. Catharines. A popular president at a university about half the size of the University of Calgary, he was an experienced hand, and was familiar with urban communities large and small.

In the course of a *Gauntlet* interview on arriving, he was also very candid about his views of the flawed methodology of the *Maclean's* university surveys, revealing, "I'm a very competitive guy, and that's what bothers me about *Maclean's*; we don't get to play the game … if they used good measures, the U of C would do better. However, that would cost *Maclean's* more money." He also revealed that he was a big sports fan, had already met the football team, and had given them words of encouragement. In his own sporting life, he was a hockey goalie, and his teammates called him "the Sieve." He disproved this later, as his competitive instincts came to the fore when he blanked all shooters, faculty, students and staff at a fund-raiser for Dinosaur Athletics.[43]

For White, a first-class contemporary education constituted "the development of thinking skills and a broad-based interdisciplinary approach to problem recognition

President White receives Italian Ambassador. Valeria Lee, Italian Studies on right. UC 2001.037.09.01.

and solving; and flexibility." Thinking, learning, and creating were the new basics of the information society. He welcomed a future then with problems to be solved, since they were but "great opportunities disguised as insoluble problems." [44]

The university was plunged into another cycle of strategic planning for both the short and long term. First, the university library needed fixing; and 1997 became the "Year of the Library" after the university task force, chaired by Dr. Chris Archer, concluded that "the library has been seriously under-funded and requires significant reinvestment in the collections budget as well as an increase in the number of professional librarians."[45] By the end of 1997, over $600,000 had been spent on restoring cancelled periodicals alone. By late 1998, the president could announce that $2 million had been spent on "getting the library back where it needed to be."[46]

The next step was to move forward with the plans for Strategic Direction, an approach that involved a revamping of the curriculum and the identification by GFC of the seven elements of a core curriculum across more than a hundred academic programs. The Academic Program Committee of GFC tackled the issue of direct entry to faculties in some way that would involve an assessment of the pre-program year in General Studies. The other major renovation suggested was the creation of four super-faculties from the current sixteen, placed in clusters of affinity. The rationale was the trimming of administrative costs and the more efficient and flexible allocation of resources. The discussion centred on the shape of the four clusters, one model being Science and Engineering; Health Sciences; Arts and Community Development; and Management; with other variations on the themes.[47] About half of the deans saw no need to change the current diverse mix, so the president created a Hearing Panel of twelve, chaired by Dr. Marvin Fritzler from Medicine, to hear the arguments pro and con Strategic Transformation.[48]

The Hearing Panel reported to GFC on February 19, 1998 and announced the creation of five strategic groups: namely, Health Sciences (Kinesiology, Nursing, Medicine, Social Work); Science and Technology (Engineering, Science, Environmental Design); Humanities and Arts (Fine Arts, General Studies, Social Sciences, Humanities); and Management and Law (Law, Management). Added to these super-faculties were the Graduate Studies and Continuing Education Faculties, which had a unique role. The rationale, as the president noted in his open paper to the faculty, was to put the faculties together in synergistic ways to "support collaborative ventures that transcend boundaries between faculties, departments and other units...."[49] The president was team-building and socializing the deans in clusters of common interest, thereby eliminating much of the individualist approach to "empire building" that was a part of the growth cycle of the seventies and eighties.

Occasionally, he ran into stiff resistance. After the President's Address, Richard Heyman of Education first thanked him for his "upbeat talk" and allowed that he could "understand why you do that." Then came the 'but': "I'd like to ask you why is it that I and many of my colleagues feel that this place is going to hell in a hand

Dr. Patrick Lee, Cancer Researcher, Foothills Hospital, November, 1998. UC2001.037.09.01.

basket? I'm sorry I have to ask this kind of question. I've never known morale here to be lower." He proceeded to list the library problems, non-consultation in Education on faculty clusters, and the inability of the university to persuade the government to understand the "dire straits that the universities of Alberta are in."[50]

The president then carefully detailed his efforts in areas such as the library and appeals for budgetary increases, and addressed all the problems at hand. And he appealed for some relief from the "relentless negativity" in the media, which had aired the university's labour relations in the *Herald*, remonstrating against the sending of unmarked brown envelopes to columnists.[51] In sum, he said he took some solace in being positive, since the alternative was that "I'd go nuts in a week." Then he proudly recited the reasons why he still felt good about the university, in that it had an excellent reputation and a wonderful future ahead of it.[52]

As a trained sociologist in group dynamics in the North American tradition, White worked hard at establishing consensus, and knew that the path to a unified approach was to preserve diversity. He was a tireless promoter, whether it was through the committee structure or through direct encouragement of the sports teams and presentation of awards to any and every worthy participant. Nor did he lose any opportunity to mention the research achievements of faculty as being second only to UBC in western Canada. Specifically, in his town hall address he lauded the cancer research breakthrough of Patrick Lee,[53] and the technical support given by the Learning Commons to teaching in 1998.[54] He and his wife Sue also followed in the tradition of the Frasers before them. They did a lot of entertaining at their home, typically "spring mixers" for GFC, and welcoming of new faculty in the fall.

White's predecessor, Murray Fraser, passed away in the spring of 1997 at the age of fifty-nine. The university had lost one of its most popular presidents, who had worked tirelessly on its behalf. There was a heartwarming celebration of his life at a packed Jack Simpson Gymnasium, with glowing accolades from the Chairman of the Board, Richard Haskayne, Chancellors Palmer and McCaig, students, and the Minister of Education. Ontario Supreme Court judge James MacPherson, a former law student, talked about how Fraser had been "ahead of his time," teaching law from an interdisciplinary perspective.[55] Tributes poured in from faculty and students registering their appreciation of Murray and Anne Fraser's work on behalf of the university, detailing their achievements, but even more praising them for remembering their names or offering lifts to the university from downtown.[56]

President White commemorated Fraser at Convocation in 1998, when he dedicated the Professional Faculties Building Block B as Fraser Hall. As Dr. White indicated, the naming was appropriate since the building housed the Law Faculty, Human Resources, and Printing Services, thus acknowledging "his scholarship in law and his concern for the people in the university community."[57] White also proceeded to appoint the university's first three presidents, Armstrong, Carrothers, and Cochrane as Presidents Emeriti. In so providing this honour, President White indicated that the Board of Governors was acknowledging "the hard and inspiring work in seeing U of C through its early years and [in] laying the foundation for the outstanding university it is today."[58]

THE CHANGING OF THE GUARD

The nineties saw the passing of the pioneers who had made the university, either by death or retirement. The debt was enormous to this group who had served wisely and well. During this time, the university said farewell to Gordon Morrison

(1928–91), a sound technician who rose to become director of the physical plant; Herman Konrad (1936–97), a long-term member of the Department of Anthropology and History and an expert on Mexican Studies; Gerry McGinley (1931–98), Bursar for a decade beginning in 1964, and then Associate Vice-President, first of Academic Administration and then of Priorities and Planning. He was honoured with the Order of the University of Calgary in 1997. George Wing (1921–98) served as Associate Dean in the Faculty of Arts and Science in the early seventies. In his retirement years, he wrote two novels – *Copperknob* and *Hector's War* – the former winning the Alberta New Fiction Competition in the early nineties. The university also paid its respects to Richard Forbis (1914–99), who with Scotty MacNeish created a new department of Archaeology, and persuaded the government to purchase Head-Smashed-In-Buffalo Jump near Fort Macleod, the current location of a major provincial museum; Amy Turek, a wonderful budget officer, who kept the fastidious books of the Science Faculty until her retirement and delighted in correcting the errors in computerized accounts as they became the mainstay; Earl Guy (1922–2005), a founding member of the Department of English and department head from 1964 to 1971; and Helen Stadelbauer (1910–2006), who first joined the staff of the Normal School and then the Calgary Branch. She went to Columbia on an unpaid leave to earn her Bachelors and Masters Degrees in Art, rejoined Calgary in 1949, and worked towards building an Art Department comparable to the larger universities in the USA.

Many retirement occasions were also held during the nineties and beyond for early and normal retirements of those with thirty years more or less with the university. Some notables were Bob Church, who became a Member of the Order of Canada as a Professor Emeritus in 2000 in honour of his work in science and industry.[59] Another of the emeriti to be so honoured by the Order of Canada was music composer and first Dean of Fine Arts, Richard Johnston. At the age of eighty, he was still proclaiming, "The arts endure; they don't go out of fashion."[60] The administration of the university was turning over, as new deans and department heads regularly came and went. Long-standing veteran Michael Maher, who was Dean of Management for eighteen years, moved on in 1999.[61] So did Alan Macdonald, who departed in the same year after twenty years in office, and service in numerous capacities as University Orator and Director of Libraries, the University Press, and other special task forces.[62] Another of the enduring servants of the university, Gary Krivy, stepped down after thirty-seven years in the Registrar's Office, eighteen of them as Registrar.[63]

THE MILLENNIUM AND A NEW AGE

The university continued to struggle with provincial grants reduced from 4 percent annual growth to 2 percent in the latter days of the White administration in 2000–2001, not enough to balance a budget with even modest salary increases. With the tuition increases pushing the annual cost of students' education from $1,500 to $4,000 in ten years, and the consequent student protests becoming "quite intense and personal by 1999," the president let it be known that he was not going to seek a second term in 2000. As he said later, "Thirteen years is long enough as a university president," particularly if one adds eight more as a dean of a large faculty, the size of a small university.[64] It was time for a change, but the university celebrated White's achievements of the previous five years. They were considerable: new residence capacity at Cascade Hall in the expansion for 400 more students; a new Information and Computer Technology? (ICT) building for computer innovation; the acquisition of the west campus from the provincial government, and the planning of the Alberta Children's Hospital; the Learning Commons and the Weekend University; the core curriculum, Strategic Directions and Transformation, and the faculty clusters. It was a record of which, the Board Chair Ted Newall indicated, one could be proud: Terry White "has changed this university and set us on a path to becoming one of North America's top research and teaching universities."[65]

The millennium had been ushered in, and after a brief time of holding their breath, people found that the world had neither come to an end nor had "Y2K"

disabled all the information systems in North America and Europe. Much of the latter reprieve was attributed to careful planning to avert disaster. The University of Calgary had its own Year 2000 Project, which coordinated efforts of faculties and departments to address areas of concern such as information technology, embedded systems, and supply chains.[66] All computer-based systems, such as the heating system, utilities, and tele- communications systems were monitored by the university and the city of Calgary to avoid any disruption of service. Disaster planning and back-up plans in case of service disruptions were initiated along with the usual remediation and testing of current systems and operations. Y2K was a much anticipated apocalyptic event, but it soon faded into millennial optimism about the future of humankind once January 1, 2000 rolled around.[67]

The university also had to select a new leader for the first years of the century and millennium, and he proved to be a highly articulate Vice-President (Academic) from McMaster University, Dr. Harvey Weingarten. In his first interview, the new president was forthright in maintaining that the university was a large group of "very good talented people," and that the main challenge would be "recruiting and retaining the best and right people" of both faculty and staff. The second challenge was to "use our resources wisely and strategically ... and use them in a way that promotes the goals of the institution." As to planning and implementation, he had the sense that there was much of the former at the U of C, but that there was "a need to help with implementation." In short, "the greatest plans in the world are not helpful unless they are implemented. That will be one of my tasks." Indeed it was, and he set out both to plan and to realize the plans in his term of office.[68]

After eight months of planning, writing, and discussion, where Vice-President Academic Ron Bond, carried revisions back and forth to deans and department heads probably ten times, the academic plan, "Raising our Sights," was presented to General Faculties Council and unanimously adopted on April 18, 2002.[69] According to the president, he now had "a roadmap for moving forward" in the next four years, and could provide a framework for preferential allocation of resources. The four core principles in the plan were enduring ones: (1) learning-centred university (2) research university (3) multi-disciplinary inquiry and scholarship (4) return to community. Apart from the guiding emphasis on quality, the plan laid out a number of strategic priorities to guide its allocation of resources, such as areas of strength and comparative advantage, external support available, and potential growth at an international and national level. Having done this, the academic plan asserted that the area needn't be an established department, and identified four such themes woven through the university structures. Those selected were: (1) leading innovation in Energy and the Environment; (2) Understanding Human Behavior, Institutions, and Cultures; (3) Creating Technologies and Managing Information for the Knowledge Society; and

Ronald B. Bond, VP Academic, photo by Ken Bendiktsen.

President Weingarten at sod-turning
for the Campus Calgary Digital Library
(opposite), photo by Stuart Gradon.

(4) Advancing Health and Wellness. To promote these ends, a five-point action program was formed to raise the level of the graduate student body to 20 percent by 2006, and raise the PhD component as well; raise the quality of the undergraduate students; integrate the four core principles with academic and support staff recruitment and retention; integrate the four core principles with the entire program and administrative structures of the university; and last, emphasize post-degree credentials along with regular degrees as the primary form of lifelong learning at the University.[70]

It was an integrated plan to set the bar higher at the university, and the next step was the roadmap. "Where Do We Go From Here?" was the subject of the president's annual address to GFC in the fall of 2002. With performance indicators in place and the goals set, the president announced increases in the graduate complement of 16 to 50 percent, depending on the area, and an increase of the undergraduate admission averages to 81.2 percent. About nine faculties admitted students directly into the first year, some above that average and some below, but the trend was up.[71] Still saddled with only a 2 percent budget increase,[72] Weingarten asked the Science faculty a month later, "How do we reduce spending and improve quality at the same time?" His answer in brief was, "We will invest more resources in those areas where we can have the greatest impact on improving the quality of education and research."[73] It was clearly, as Vice-President Bond reflected, "an academic plan with teeth," and he and the budget committee had the signal to discriminate.[74]

At the same time, the student body rose to the thirty thousand mark, while the budget increases in the operating grant still lagged at the $200 million mark.[75] The university throttled back its intake the next year, while the operating grant still ticked up towards the $220 million mark. The government by this time was close to eliminating its debt, and with an election in the offing, times were getting better.[76] By 2005–6, the university had entered good times again, with 6 percent budgetary increases in the operating grant promised for a three-year window.[77]

Fund-raising was steadily becoming easier in the heady economic climate Alberta was enjoying, and from 2004 to 2006 a total of $13.6 million was added in new student scholarships, raising the total scholarship support to $43.5 million from $28 million in 2004. Overall fund-raising was also increasing, from $18 million in 2003, to $63 million in 2004, to $80 million in 2006, exceeding its $70 million target. This included the largest-ever gift of $25 million by Seymour Schulich to the Faculty of Engineering in 2005. Equally, research grants totaled $247 million in 2005, and put the University in the top ten universities in the country, the so-called "G10" of Canadian universities. The increases were highly significant, in that sponsored research through grants now represented some 27 percent of the total university budget, and accounted for much of the net increase of 225 faculty from 2001 to 2004–5.

All of a sudden, the floodgates were opened in a way they hadn't been for a very long time. Plans were in progress for a veterinary school and a new dean was recruited to begin hiring new staff in 2005–6. A sod-breaking ceremony was held in April for the building of the Digital Library, which will incur, with building and renovation of the main library and retrofitting across campus, a cost of $113 million. The list of other ventures includes the setting aside in the operating budget funds in the order of $10 million for the hiring in 2006–7 of 125 new professors; $1.75 million on merit scholarships to entice bright students; and $1.3 million towards teaching development.[78] Overall, the university budget came in

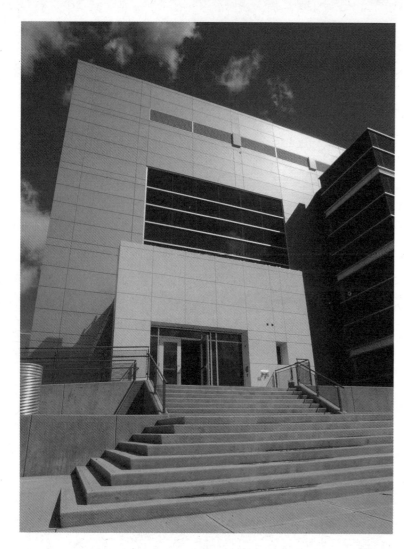

CCIT Building, photo by David Brown.

at $801 million dollars. To add to the euphoria of spring, there was an announcement of a ten-year capital plan for new and renovated facilities in the order of $1.2 billion for the University of Calgary.

High among the university's priorities was an Institute for Sustainable Energy and Energy Studies (ISEEE) Building, which would be a six-faculty collaboration on an Institute for Sustainable Energy and multidisciplinary Energy Studies Program.[79] It would also, in the view of the planners and the president, fit nicely into the plan envisioned for an experiential learning centre for students.[80] Another visible enthusiasm of the president and the planning group was the urban campus plan for the East Village near City Hall. It was hoped that this "Urban Campus Initiative," a joint project of the U of C, Athabasca University, Bow Valley College, Chinook Learning, and SAIT would be able to open some 2500 university spaces in its $205 million budget. The city was involved in the selection of a 750,000 ASM site in Ward Seven, since the urban campus would undoubtedly bring renewed vitality to the area.[81]

The trickle-down effects of such enterprise and planning were visible in what was possible in the new order, but was not a decade or even a half-decade before. Witness the Faculty of Engineering and the career of its Dean, Chan Wirasinghe, who assumed the deanship in its darkest hour of budget cuts in 1994 and retired in 2006, just after the Schulich gift to the faculty, and its renaming as The Schulich School of Engineering. As he indicated, he was not in 1994 about to "sit around cutting the school by twenty percent," so he tried to figure out how to move the school ahead while finessing the cuts.[82] The first thing was to try to get more women in the engineering school. Wirasinghe asked a colleague, Dr. David Irvine-Halliday, to set up a Women in Engineering committee, and he committed himself

Chan Wirasinghe, Dean of Engineering,
photo by Stuart Gradon.

entirely to a continuous planning process, to establishing clear communications with community stakeholders, and to improving the quality of faculty.

The results were incrementally satisfying, with the Chairs Program moved from half a research chair in the eighties to more than thirty in twelve years, the most in western Canada, and the most research funding per faculty member as well.[83] There were other visible reminders of growth in the two new buildings, CCIT and ICT, plus more to come with the capital expansion planned for the next ten years. The larger impact for the university was not lost upon the veteran dean. "If you look at the evolution of great universities you'll see that they didn't become great because all their faculties were great. By luck, or circumstance, or design, certain faculties become prominent and that light shines on the whole university.... If we can choose some winners and really support them, everybody else will be supported automatically. If the reputation of the school goes up, then the university's reputation also goes up."[84]

The effects of boom times are spreading across campus to more than the professional faculties, the natural recipients of government and corporate largesse. The digital library project is another case in point. When complete in three years, it will become part of the Campus Alberta Lois Hole Digital Library. It is a multi-partner enterprise spread across several campuses, and it depends on the inter-institutional co-operation of the universities and colleges of Alberta. Two key players in the universities in developing digitization projects in the past decade have been Ernie Ingles, Chief Librarian at the University of Alberta, and Frits Pannekoek, the Director of Information Services at the University of Calgary from 1999 to 2005.[85]

The university has come a long way in forty years, but in a sense has come back to the point where it started, autonomous with seemingly unlimited capital for building and hiring. It is a time to share some of that pioneering spirit, that enterprise which has built the campus from several hundred acres of virgin prairie into a thriving hub of activity and ideas. It could not have been done without any one of the presidents, faculties, support units, departments, or sports teams, for it is an organism of great complexity in which all have had a share. It was truly an astonishing achievement in four mere decades, fuelled mainly by black gold beneath the prairie and northern forest, and also by the intellectual energy and collective effort on the surface that brought it so far and so fast in less than two generations.

NOTES

NOTES TO CHAPTER ONE

1 Douglas Owram, ed., *The Formation of Alberta: A Documentary History* (Edmonton: Alberta Records Publication Board/ Alberta Historical Society, 1979), 379–96. For other histories of this early period, see Robert M. Stamp, *Becoming a Teacher in 20th Century Calgary: A History of the Normal School and the Faculty of Education, University of Calgary* (Calgary: Detselig Enterprises, 2004), Ch. 1, 11–27; A.W. Rasporich, "The University of Calgary's Pre-History, 1912–66," *Alberta History*, 54, no. 3 (Summer 2006): 2–11.

2 James Gray, *R.B. Bennett: The Calgary Years* (Toronto: University of Toronto Press, 1991), 49.

3 Donald B. Smith, "Calgary's First Fight 75 Years Old," *Calgary Herald*, 3 October 1987.

4 See *The Morning Albertan*, Calgary, 10 April 1912, 8.

5 D.B. Smith, *Calgary Herald*, 3 October 1987.

6 Smith, *Calgary Herald*, 3 October 1987 and Calgary *Standard*, 28 September 1912, vol. 2, no. 24, "Opening of the University of Calgary."

7 See *Calgary Herald*, 26 September 1913, reporting Alberta Legislature debates of 24 September on the Speech from the Throne.

8 Sage left after two years for Queen's University and then the University of British Columbia, where he had a long and distinguished career. He later wrote an account of the demise of the first university in Calgary, "Calgary College, 1912–15," Glenbow Archives, M7699, Sage-Mackinnon Family Fonds. The most comprehensive history to be written was by Norman MacLeod, "Calgary College, 1912–15: A Study of an Attempt to Establish a Privately Financed University in Alberta" (Unpublished PhD Thesis, University of Calgary, 1970); see also Phyllis Weston, "A University for Calgary," *Alberta Historical Review* 11, no. 3 (Summer 1963): 1–11.

9 Calgary *Western Standard*, 28 September, 5 October, 7 October, 24 October 1913.

10 See E.A. Corbett, *Henry Marshall Tory: A Biography*, 2nd ed. (Edmonton: University of Alberta Press, 1992), 121.

11 Alberta, *Report of the Commission Appointed to Consider the Granting of Degree-Conferring Powers to Calgary College* (1915), Sessional Papers, no.1, (Edmonton: J.W. Jeffrey, 1915).

12 Glenbow Archives, Sage-MacKinnon Family Fonds, Walter Sage, "Calgary College," 4.

13 University of Calgary Archives, UARC 00.003. Calgary Normal School Papers, Irvine Grahame interview, 1987.

14 *Ibid*, UARC JO.003, Calgary Normal School Papers.

15 Douglas Coats, "Calgary: The Private Schools, 1900–16," in H.C. Klassen and A.W. Rasporich, eds., *Frontier Calgary: Town, City and Region, 1874–1914* (Calgary: McClelland and Stewart West, 1975), 49.

16 Harry Sanders, "The Struggle to Establish a University in Calgary: Historical Timeline," (Calgary: unpublished ms., n.d.), 7, 24.

17 *Calgary Herald*, 14 February 1946.

18 *Calgary Herald*, 21 February 1946; UARC 68.003, Calgary University Committee Papers, Minutes, 19 March 1946.

19 *Herald*, 21 February 1946.

20 *Herald*, 8 March 1946.

21 University of Calgary Archives, UARC, 88.02. Faculty of Education Minutes, Faculty of the Council of Education, Calgary Branch, 12 April 1951, 67.

22 UARC, 88.025, Department of History University History Papers, Ethel King-Shaw interview transcript, 13 June 1990, 2.

23 William F. Reid, "Crisis in Education," *The Alberta School Trustee* 17(4) (April 1947): 24–25.

24 *Calvette,* 16 February 1955.

25 H. Sanders, "The Struggle…Timeline," 55–58.

26 City of Calgary Archives, City Clerk's Papers, Don MacKay, Mayor, to Andrew Stewart, 27 September 1955; ibid, A. Stewart to E. Bredin, City Solicitor, 9 April 1956; ibid, E. Bredin to Carl Cummer, 8 April 1957.

27 UARC 00.004, University of Alberta Board of Governors' Reports, Reports for 1957-58 (p. 14), Reports for 1958–59. City of Calgary Archives, City Clerk's Papers, A. Stewart to Don McKay, 6 October 1958.

28 F. Terentiuk interview by Robert Bott, 1990; Tim Christison, May 2006.

29 Robert Bott, *The University of Calgary: A Place of Vision* (Calgary: University of Calgary Press, 1990), 20. Johns was later to record the echoes of the earlier failure of Calgary College in his report to the University of Alberta Board of Governors, "It may, in the view of some, be fifty years too late." UARC 00.004, U of A Board of Governors Reports, 1961–62, President Walter Johns' Report, 11.

30 Robert Stamp, *Becoming a Teacher*, 74.

31 Norman Wardlaw, reminiscence of Tom Oliver, 6 October 1997, 12, courtesy Finley Campbell.

32 Peter Krueger interview by Robert Bott, 1990; by A.W. Rasporich, March 2006.

33 See *Calgary Herald*, 27 October 1960; "4 Million Dollar Job Finished in Less than Two Years."

34 University of Calgary Archives, C.J. McLaurin, "What is the Future for the University of Alberta," University of Calgary: Fall Convocation Address, 17 November 1961, (Calgary: C.O. Nickle Publications, Calgary), 2 pp.

35 University of Calgary Archives, Banff Planning Conference, 1961.

36 R.M. Stamp, *Becoming a Teacher*, 82–83.

37 Ibid., 87.

38 Donald Mills, "Reflections on the Early Years," cited in Harry Hiller, *First Forty: Sociology at the University of Calgary, 1963-2003* (Calgary: Department of Sociology, 2003), 18–21.

39 Quentin and Joyce Doolittle, interview with Tim Christison, January 2006. Victor Mitchell, email to Tim Christison, 16 January 2006.

40 Peter Lancaster, "Ruby Memories," Winter 2006.

41 Hyne interview transcript, 29 June 1990.

42 Finley Campbell interview by A.W. Rasporich, April 2006.

43 R.M. Stamp, *Becoming a Teacher*, 87.

44 Gordon Nelson interview by Tim Christison, May 2006.

45 See Marci McDonald, "The Man Behind Stephen Harper," *The Walrus Magazine,* 2005.

46 M. Yacowar, e-mail to Tim Christison, 16 January 2006.

47 *Gauntlet*, 28 October 1960.

48 *Gauntlet*, 11 November 1960.

49 Yacowar to Christison, 16 January 2006.

50 *Gauntlet*, 21 September 1973. "Corbet Locke Is Here to Stay."

51 Ibid.

52 *UC Gazette*, 15 October 1968.

53 Rod Wittig interview by A.W. Rasporich, May 2006.

54 *UC Gazette*, 15 October 1985.

55 *UC Gazette,* 15 October 1985.

56 See *Calgary Herald*, 25 March 2006, Section A3.

57 *Calgary Herald*, 7, 8 November 1963.

58 *On Campus*, 13 January 2006.

59 Gordon Nelson interview with T.Christison, May 2006; also F. Terentiuk interview with Tim Christison, May 2006.

60 Victor Mitchell e-mail to Tim Christison, 16 January 2006.

61 *Calgary Herald,* 17 December 1965.

62 *Calgary Herald*, 12 December 1963.

63 UARC 88.025 Hyne interview transcript, 29 June 1990, J.B., 1–2.

64 *Calgary Herald*, 1 November 1963.

65 *Calgary Herald*, 1 November 1963. Johns' trenchant views on Calgary expansion and its expense were periodically expressed in negative terms, such as the letter he wrote to A.L. Doucette in December 1959, in which he indicated Calgary's enrolment numbers were inflated and demands for library facilities were excessive. Further he stated, "Certain departments will be developed to serve Calgary and the Southern part of the province, but we cannot attempt to duplication the expensive facilities of the campus in Edmonton for many years to come." Doucette Papers, University of Calgary Archives, file 20.01.

66 UARC, 68.003, Calgary University Committee Papers, Statements of C.J. McLaurin, late 1964, 2.

67 *Calgary Herald*, 15 November 1963.

NOTES TO CHAPTER TWO

1 For a general context to this period, see Doug Owram, *Born at the Right Time: A History of the Baby Boom Generation* (Toronto; University of Toronto Press, 1996), 111–248.

2 See Donald Mills," Reminiscence," in Harry H. Hiller, *First Forty: Sociology At The University Of Calgary* (University of Calgary, 2003), 18–19; R.M. Stamp, *Becoming a Teacher in the 20th Century; A History of the Calgary Normal School and the Faculty of Education*, (University of Calgary: Detselig Enterprises, 2004), 81.

3 *Gauntlet*, 10 March 1967.

4 Peter G. Glockner, *A Place of Ingenuity: The Faculty of Engineering* (Calgary: University of Calgary Printing Services, 1994), 28.

5 Stamp, *Becoming a Teacher*, 88.

6 Stamp, 87. UARC 66.002, General Faculty Council, *Minutes*, 3 September 1966.

7 Vernon Jones and George Lane, "Development by Design: A History of the Faculty of Management at the University of Calgary, 1967–91," in Barbara Austin, *Capitalizing Knowledge: Essays on the History of Business Education in Canada* (Toronto: University of Toronto Press, 2000), 209–38.

8 Jones and Lane, "Development by Design," 211.

9 UARC 68.003, Calgary University Committee Papers, *Minutes*, 2 February 1955.

10 UARC 82.001, Armstrong Papers, Minutes of the Board of Governors of the University of Alberta, 1 May 1964, 9.

11 UARC 82.001, Armstrong Papers, Speech to the 2nd Annual Convention, Canadian Association of Medical Clinics, 6 May 1966, 1.

12 See UARC 66.002, General Faculty Council, Agreement between the University of Alberta, Calgary, and the Foothills Provincial General Hospital, Diploma Program in Nursing, November 1964.

13 Geertje Boschma, *Faculty of Nursing on the Move: Nursing at the University of Calgary, 1969–2004* (Calgary: University of Calgary Press, 2005), 31.

14 UARC 88.025, Finley Campbell interview ms., 18 May 1990.

15 UARC 88.025, Fred Terentiuk interview ms., 18 May 1990; G. Boschma, *Faculty of Nursing*, 37–48.

16 See *Gauntlet*, "Medics Could Suffer," 18 October 1967.

17 W.A. Cochrane interview with the author, April 2006.

18 UARC 88.025, W.A. Cochrane interview by Robert Bott, 6 June 1990, 3.

19 *Gauntlet*, 18 October 1967.

20 UARC 88.025, Cochrane interview, 6 June 1990.

21 *History of the Campus* (University of Calgary; Physical Plant, March 1992), 11.

22 Stamp, *Becoming a Teacher*, 88–91.

23 *History of the Campus*, 11.

24 *Gauntlet*, 31 January 1968.

25 G.Boschma, *Faculty of Nursing on the Move*, 37–38.

26 *UC Gazette*, 14 December 1998, commenting on a story by Frits Pannekoek, Director of Information Resources, in ibid., 30 November 1998.

27 *Gauntlet*, 25 November, 1975

28 *Gauntlet,* 4 October 1974.

29 Rod Wittig interview with author, May 2006.

30 Gerry McGinley discussion with author, n.d.

31 See *UC Gazette*, 11 April 1988, 10 July 85; 16 August 1973.

32 UARC 88.025, Bob Church interview, 6 June 1990.

33 D. Balzer, "Dustbowl Days are Over: How the University of Calgary Campus rose from the dust in just 40 years," *AlbertaViews* (January/February 2002): 42–49.

34 *UC Gazette*, 18 September 1975.

35 *Gauntlet*, 3 December 1975.

36 Peter Krueger interview with the author, February 2006.

37 *UC Gazette*, 13 November 1973.

38 *Gauntlet*, 19 April 1973.

39 *Gauntlet,* 15 November 1973.

40 *Gauntlet,* 15 July 1971; 15 March 1973.'

41 UARC 88.025, J.B. Hyne interview transcript, 1990, 6.

42 J.B. Hyne Comments for Deans' Council, 82.001.II (2). See also J.B. Hyne to Herb Armstrong, 25 March 1968, re: visit of Mr. Ferne of OECD, 7 pp.

43 Additional committees were established to report on research in the universities in Canada, e.g., the Macdonald Committee in 1967, "Support of Research in Universities," 10 January 1968, WR Trost, VP (Academic), 21 pp.

44 University of Alberta Archives, Walter Johns to Herb Armstrong, 29 December 1966, 69-123-473.

45 "University of Calgary Library and Information Resources – A Timeline," unpublished ms., 4.

46 "Student Activism," *Gauntlet*, 15 October 1969.

47 "Student Activism," *Gauntlet*, 22 October 1969. "Panther Speech Sparks Heated Debate."

48 "Student Activism," *Gauntlet*, 14 September 1970.

49 "Student Activism," *Gauntlet*, 26 February 1969.

50 "Student Activism," *Gauntlet*, 1 September 1971.

51 *Gauntlet*, 1 September 1971, "A Mythological History of the U of C."

52 M. Nowakowski, reminiscence, 28 February 2006 to T.Christison. See also *Gauntlet*, 15 March 1974, 3, "Speakers Corner's Loss. Ed Hamel-Shey passed away at a young age in Vancouver on Monday, 11 March 1974." For *Gauntlet* editors and reporters of this period, see "Where Are the Gauntleteers Now?" *Gauntlet*, 20th Anniversary Issue. Mention is made of Kevin Peterson, 1967–68, Pat Tivy, 1972–73 and other writers who later worked for the Calgary *Herald*, like Geoff White, Bob Bragg and Allan Connery.

53 *Gauntlet*, 1 December 1971.

54 W.M. Stewart at GFC, cited in *UC Gazette*, 18 October 1972.

55 *UC Gazette*, 18 October 1972. For a student recollection, see "Anarchy at the U of C" (re: James Prescott), *Gauntlet*, 9 November 1995, 8.

56 *Gauntlet*, 25 November 1973.

NOTES TO CHAPTER THREE

1 Peter Smith, "Urban Development Trends in the Prairie Provinces," in A.W. Rasporich, *The Making of the Modern West: Western Canada Since 1945* (Calgary: University of Calgary Press, 1984), 133–45;.Max Foran, *Calgary: An Illustrated History,* (Toronto: Lorimer/National Museums of Canada, 1978), Ch. 4.

2 John J. Barr, "The Impact of Oil on Alberta: Retrospect and Prospect," in Rasporich, *The Making of the Modern West,* 97–105.

3 Michael J. McMordie, "The Interdisciplinary History of Interdisciplinary Education: University of Calgary's Faculty of Environmental Design," unpublished ms., 22 October 2004, 7; Gordon Nelson interview by Tim Christison, May 2006.

4 W.T. Perks e-mail to Tim Christison, April 2006.

5 *Gauntlet*, 17 February 1971.

6 McMordie, "Interdisciplinary History," 4–5, citing letter read to GFC Meeting #58, 9 December 1972. *Minutes* 58.5.1 (e).

7 McMordie, 7–8. Walter Johns, *A History of the University of Alberta, 1906–69* (Edmonton: University of Alberta Press, 1981), 473. Johns stated, "The reaction of our GFC was to ask the Board of Governors to use every legal means possible to reverse the commission's decision. Nevertheless the decision stood."

8 *Gauntlet*, 6 December 1972, 7. For an especially militant view of Canadianization in this period, see Robin Matthews, "No Canadians Need Apply," *UBC Chronicle* (Autumn 1974): 21. Matthews took special pains to identify the hostile reactions of the presidents of the universities of Calgary and Alberta to Canadianization to the Moir Commission.

9 *Gauntlet*, 15 November 1972.

10 *Gauntlet*, 25 March 1977.

11 *UC Gazette,* 27 September 1979; 10 January 1980.

12 See Ian A.L. Getty and Donald B. Smith, *One Century Later: Western Canadian Reserve Indians Since Treaty 7* (Vancouver: UBC Press, 1978).

13 R.M. Stamp, *Becoming a Teacher*, 100.

14 *Gauntlet*, 23 October 1973.

15 *Gauntlet*, 9 September 1975.

16 See *UC Gazette*, 16 May 1974.

17 See Marsha Hanen, "Some Thoughts on Interdisciplinarity Then and Now" presented at the 20th Anniversary Celebration of the Faculty of General Studies, University of Calgary, 10 May 2001.

18 See *Gauntlet*, 23 February 1972; 1 February 1974 ; 16 March 1976.

19 See K. Glazier, *The Story of My Life*, 16.

20 Glazier, *The Story of My Life*, 36. See also *UC Gazette*, 9 May 1973.

21 Glazier, *The Story of My Life*, 7 March 1978, 6.

22 K. Glazier, *The Story of My Life*, 37.

23 *Gauntlet*, 12 September 1972.

24 *Gauntlet,* 22 March 1972.

25 See *Gauntlet*, 10 January 1973, "Carrothers wins budget boost" (9.3%).

26 University of Calgary *Academic Plan, 1972*, 2.

27 *Academic Plan*, 2.

28 *Academic Plan*, 3.

29 *Academic Plan*, 7.

30 *Academic Plan,* 6.

31 *Gauntlet*, 7 September 1973.

32 Finley Campbell, "Toast to Fred and Jane Carrothers on Leaving the University of Calgary," unpublished ms. provided to author, June 1974.

33 *UC Gazette*, 17 October 1974.

34 John McLaren interview with Tim Christison, May 2006.

35 McLaren interview and *Gauntlet*, 11 June 1975, "Law School Departs from Tradition," 5.

36 *UC Gazette*, 3 October 1974. Installation Address.

37 R.M Stamp, *Becoming a Teacher*, 98.

38 *Gauntlet* date?? 1; "Education: A Faculty of Incompetence," 17 September 1974, 6; "Education Faculty Investigated," 4 June 1975, l.

39 *UC Gazette*, 29 May 1975; R.M. Stamp, *Becoming a Teacher*, 98

40 See *Gauntlet*, "Task force slams Education faculty, 7 April 1976, l.

41 R.M. Stamp, *Becoming a Teacher*, 104.

42 Stamp, *Becoming a Teacher*, 106.

43 *Gauntlet*, 25 June 1975.

44 See *Gauntlet*, 21 January 1977, for Social Welfare and response by Dean Tim Tyler on 4 November 1977. For Science, see ibid., 19 January 1978).

45 Penelhum interview with J. Dickin, *Gauntlet*, 10 March 1967.

46 *UC Gazette*, 14 January 1972.

47 As he said on leaving in 1975, "You find 99% of your time is spent solving problems raised by others … you can't be both Dean … and engage in academic work." *Gauntlet*, 4 June 1975, 3.

48 *Gauntlet*, 14 March 1975.

49 *Gauntlet*, 4 April 1975.

50 *Gauntlet*, 8 September 1976.

51 *Gauntlet,* 1 October 1976.

52 *Gauntlet*, 27 September 1977.

53 *UC Gazette,* 28 October 1976.

54 Ron Franklin, conversation, 12 June 2006; see also *UC Gazette*, 7 September 1993.

55 Canadian Energy Research Institute, Chronology, unpublished ms., 1.

56 Canadian Energy Research Institute, Chronology, Carrrothers to Bill Dickie, 12 December 1971.

57 See CERI Historical Chronology, 5 pp., courtesy F.A. Campbell.

58 Robert Macdonald, "Challenges and Accomplishments: A Celebration of the Arctic Institute of North America," *Arctic* 58, no. 4 (December 2005): 446.

59 W.R.N. Blair to W.A. Cochrane, 76-03-24. GFC 122.4.2 *Minutes*.

60 *UC Gazette*, 26 June 1980, 1.

61 See *UC Gazette*, 7 August 1980. See his later involvement in CACI, *UC Gazette*, 11 February 1987.

62 UARC 88.025, J.B. Hyne interview, 1990.

63 *UC Gazette*, 11 July 1988, 6.

64 *UC Gazette*, 30 October 1980.

65 See Report of University Press Publications Subcomitee, 1976, 11–24.

66 See *Gauntlet*, 17 September 1980; *UC Gazette*, 11 September 1980.

67 See *UC Infoserve*, 13, no. 1 (March 2006): 4–5.

68 See e.g. *UC Gazette*, passim: F. Campbell, 3 June 1971, FRSC; P.J. Krueger, Herzberg Award, 21 November 1973; J.B. Hyne, Gordon Drummond, Alberta Achievement Awards, 4 November 1980 ; R. de Paiva, Fellow of the Institution of Stuctural Engineers,London, 21 August 1980.

69 *UC Gazette,* 11 December 1980. Program Review Committee was established in 1979, composed of eight senior academics who would evaluate overall university development, each committee member analyzing the programs of two faculties. The report was called, upon its release late in 1980, *The Shrinking Maze*, a metaphor the president explained in this way: "Every maze, though it poses challenges and choices along the way, offers the prospect of hard-won achievement to those who negotiate it successfully."

NOTES TO CHAPTER FOUR

1 Palmer and Palmer, *Alberta,* 353.

2 *Gauntlet*, 6 April 1979, 1.

3 See Jim Stanford, "Cutbacks: The Saga Continues," *Gauntlet*, 7 October 1981, 9.

4 *Calgary Herald*, 25 March 2005, Observer Section, A3.

5 See "Nickle Art Museum $500,000 to fall short," *Gauntlet*, 7 December 1977.

6 See *UC Gazette*, 18 January 1979, 1, 4. Dean Alan Robertson of Fine Arts was critical of the university and the Nickle for ignoring the needs of his faculty. *Gauntlet*, 1 April 1982, 3.

7 *Gazette*, 30 May 1984.

8 V. Jones and G. Lane, "History of the Faculty of Management…" 220.

9 R. Schulz interview, 2006. *UC Gazette*, 12 March 1981.

10 *UC Gazette*, 22 August 1988; *Gauntlet*, 30 November 1989.

11 See *UC Gazette,* 9 September 1993, "Professional Faculties Building."

12 *UC Gazette*, 26 February 1981.

13 *UC Gazette*, 2 April 1981.

14 Interview, Cathy Wagner with T. Christison, April 2006.

15 *UC Gazette*, 22 April 1982. Interview, Fred Terentiuk with Tim Christison, May 2006.

16 *UC Gazette* 5 October 1981.

17 *UC Gazette* 5 October 1981.

18 See *History of the Campus*, 12.

19 *Gauntlet*, 6 September 1984.

20 *Gauntlet* 19 November 1987.

21 *Gazette*, 6 March 1985.

22 *Gauntlet*, 4 December 1981.

23 *Gazette*, 11 October 1986.

24 Robert G. Weyant, "On the Care and Feeding of an Infant Faculty" Talk presented at the symposium on "Paradigms Lost and Paradigms Gained; Negotiating Interdisciplinarity in the Twenty-First Century," The Faculty of Communications and Culture of the University of Calgary," 10 May 2001. Unpublished ms., 8 pp.

25 Weyant, "Care and Feeding," 5.

26 Weyant, "Care and Feeding," 8.

27 Alan Robertson, *Those Who Can*, 112–13.

28 *UC Gazette*, 1 April 1982.

29 Robertson, *Those Who Can*, 114.

30 Robertson, *Those Who Can*, 116.

31 Robertson, *Those Who Can*, 74–75. A slightly different version appeared in the *Gazette*, 9 October 1985.

32 *UC Gazette*, 29 January 1986.

33 From a Celebration of the Life of T.A. Oliver, 6 October 1997, unpublished ms., courtesy of F.A. Campbell.

34 *UC Gazette*, 1 April 1982.

35 *UC Gazette*, 26 June 1985.

36 *UC Gazette*, 14 September 1983.

37 *Library ... Timeline*, 14.

38 *UC Gazette,* 3 December 1981.

39 *UC Gazette*, 2 October 1985.

40 Interviews, Jan Roseneder (Library) and John Heintz (Philosophy), 2006.

41 *UC Gazette*, 30 May 1988.

42 Alan MacDonald interview with Tim Christison, 2006.

43 France Foo Fat interview with Tim Christison, 2006.

44 *On Campus*, 13 January 2006, 11.

45 Alan MacDonald interview with Tim Christison, 2006.

46 *UC Gazette*, 14 March 1988.

47 *Gauntlet,* 24 March 1988, 4.

48 *Gazette,* 3 April 1989.

49 *Gazette*, 16 May 1984.

50 *Gazette*, 29 January 1986. Hanen presented a paper to the Manitoba Historical Society on 29 October 1996, entitled "Leaps, Bounds and Baby Steps: The Changing Landscape for Women in Academic Administration," 22 pp., describing the difficult situation of women in academic administration.

51 *UC Gazette*, 21 June 1990

52 *Gauntlet*, 14 January 1981

53 *UC Gazette*, 18 January 1984, 6.

54 *Gauntlet*, 4 October 1990.

55 Gary Krivy interview with the author, February 2006.

56 *Gauntlet*, 11 January 1990.

57 See *Gauntlet*, 30 July 1992, "Native Student Centre Facing Many Challenges," re: New Director George Calliou.

58 See *Gauntlet*, 2 October 1986, in reference to GFC's discussion of the discriminatory awards the previous week.

59 *Gauntlet*, 29 October 1987.

60 *Gauntlet,* 29 October 1987.

61 *Gauntlet*, 16 February 1987, "Purge a Tory."

62 *Gauntlet,* 16 February 1987.

63 *UC Gazette*, 1 February 1988.

64 Fred Terentiuk interview with Tim Christison, May 2006.

65 See *UC Gazette,* 1 February 1986; 1 October 1986; 18 March 1987.

NOTES TO CHAPTER FIVE

1 *Gauntlet*, 17 September 1992, 4–5.

2 *UC Gazette*, 29 May 1989.

3 Ibid.

4 *Gauntlet*, 10 December 1992.

5 *UC Gazette*, 17 September 1992.

6 *Gauntlet,* 10 December 1992.

7 *Gauntlet* 10 January 1993.

8 *UC Gazette*, 31 January 1994; *Gauntlet*, 3 February 1994.

9 *Gauntlet*, 7 July 1994. The university reintroduced an early retirement program so that it would be able to meet its budgetary commitments. *UC Gazette*, 30 September 1993; *Gauntlet*, 19 May 1994.

10 *Gauntlet*, 1 April 1993: *UC Gazette*, 1 March 1993.

11 *UC Gazette*, 1 April 1991, Special Birthday Issue; 8 April 1991,"What a Party!"; see also 9 December 1991.

12 *UC Gazette*, 21 October 1991.

13 See *UC Gazette*, 15 Marc 1993, "Armstrong's Vision of the U of C Recalled."

14 Eliane Leslau Silverman, *The Last Best West: Women on the Alberta Frontier, 1880–1930,* 2nd ed. (Calgary: Fifth House, 1998), 220 pp.

15 Susan Stratton to Tim Christison, 31 January 2006.

16 *Gauntlet*, 24 October 1991.

17 *Gauntlet*, 16 July 1991, "Where Are All the Women in Science?" 3.

18 *Gazette*, 18 February 1992, 7.

19 "Recommendations," 1. Contained in Mary Valentich, *Improving the Status of Women in One University: A Report on the Decade, 1990–2000* (ms. paper to Canadian. Association for the Study of Women and Education, University of Alberta, 27–28 May 2000, 185–91.

20 *UC Gazette*, 24 June 1992.

21 T.E. Flanagan to Editor, *UC Gazette,* 19 November 1991.

22 Rainer Knopff to Editor, *UC Gazette* 13 January 1992; 10 February 1992.

23 *UC Gazette*, 13 August 1990; *Gauntlet,* 4 September 1992. See also "Sexual Harassment Advisor Remains Part-time Position, Shirley Voyna-Wilson succeeds Donna Ferrara- Kerr, *Gauntlet*, 10 December 1992.

24 *UC Gazette*, Susan Stone-Blackburn, 3 December 1990.

25 Valentich, *Improving the Status of Women*, 187; see also Mary Valentich, *Annual Report as Advisor to the President on Women's Issues*, Prepared for the President, Murray Fraser, 1 July 1993–1994, 7 pp.

26 *UC Gauntlet*, 20 June 1991, 1.

27 *UC Gazette*, 30 September 1991.

28 *UC Gazette*, 7 November 1991, 1; see also *UC Gazette*, 19 March 1992; Schulz interview with A.W. Rasporich, April 2006.

29 *UC Gazette*, 5 July 1993.

30 *UC Gazette*, 4 December 1989.

31 *UC Gazette*, 30 March 1992.

32 *UC Gazette*, 10 October 1989, "U of C now Centre of Excellence," 1.

33 *UC Gazette*, 20 April 1992.

34 *UC Gazette*, 5 July 1993.

35 *UC Gazette*, 5 July 1993.

36 *Gauntlet*, 19 March 1992.

37 *Gauntlet*, 7 November 1991.

38 GFC Meeting, 16 June 1994, but was not implemented until 11 October 1996. See *Gauntlet*, 5 September 1996, 19.

39 Robert Schulz interview with A.W. Rasporich, April 2006.

40 *UC Gazette*, 3 September 1996, 1.

41 *Gauntlet*, 30 November 1995.

42 See *Gauntlet* interview, 16 May 1996.

43 *UC Gazette*, 8 February 1999

44 *UC Gazette*, 16 October 1996.

45 *Library … timeline*, 22.

46 *UC Gazette*, 8 September 1998.

47 *UC Gazette*, 17 November 1997.

48 *UC Gazette*, 3 November 1997. Faculty Association concerns were expressed in a letter by M. Anne Stalker, *UC Gazette*, 8 December 1997, 5.

49 *UC Gazette*, 23 February 1998, 3.

50 *UC Gazette*, 6 April 1998.

51 Maurice Yacowar, Dean of Fine Arts, penned a humorous supporting letter to the editor of the *Gazette* entitled "Brown Manila Envelopes (the big mysterious kind)." It was a hilarious ten-point program in [un]ethical journalism by Rocco Stockyard, titled "How to be a Columnist (A Cram Course in Calumny)." *UC Gazette*, 20 April 1998.

52 *UC Gazette*, 6 April 1998.

53 *UC Gazette*, 17 May 1999.

54 *UC Gazette*, 6 April 1998.

55 *UC Gazette*, "I will lift up My Eyes," 24 March 1997, 1.

56 *UC Gazette*, 17 March 1997, 1–2.

57 *UC Gazette*, 19 May 1998.

58 The initiative to included these three came at the prompting of Finley Campbell, after Presidents Wagner and Fraser had been designated presidents emeriti, that the other three should be so designated; F.A. Campbell to J.E. Newell, Chair, Board of Governors, 7 November 1997. Personal copy provided to author.

59 *UC Gazette*, 24 July 2000.

60 *UC Gazette,* 30 June 1997.

61 *UC Gazette* 28 June 1999.

62 *Library… timeline*, 11–23; see "Alan MacDonald; Librarian Extraordinaire," 30 June 30 1997, honouring his receipt of the Canadian Library Association's Outstanding Service to Librarianship Award for 1997.

63 *UC Gazette*, 19 February 2002.

64 *UC Gazette*, 25 June 2001.

65 *UC Gazette*, "The White Years," Special Issue, June 2001.

66 *UC Gazette*, 22 February 1999.

67 The university sponsored several events under the logo, "Calgary 2000, It's Time," for example, talks like "Spelling the Millennium" by Dr. Hillel Schwartz, Senior Fellow of the Millennium Institute.

68 *UC Gazette*, 4 September 2001, 8.

69 *UC Gazette,* 29 April 2002.

70 *UC Gazette*, 29 April 2002, 5–7.

71 *UC Gazette*, 4 November 2002.

72 *UC Gazette*, 4 February 2002, Open Letter to the University Community, President Weingarten, 9.

73 *UC Gazette*, 16 December 2002.

74 R.B. Bond, interview with the author, April 2006.

75 President Weingarten, *Report to the Community,* 2005–6.

76 *UC Gazette*, 16 June 2003, 1, Special Budget Issue, "Moving Forward: 2003–5 Budget and Investment Priorities."

77 Bond interview, 6 April 2006; *Calgary Herald*, 20 April 2006.

78 *Calgary Herald*, 20 April 2006.

79 Bond interview with the author, 6 April 2006.

80 *UC Gazette,* H.Weingarten interview, Q&A, 16 September 2005, 4.

81 *Calgary Herald*, 8 April 2006.

82 *On Campus*, 3 March 2006.

83 *On Campus*, 3 March 2006.

84 *On Campus*, 3 March 2006.

85 *UC Gazette*, 8 September 1998.

NOTE ON SOURCES

This book is a narrative and memoir, and not, therefore, a traditional scholarly history of the university, a book that should be written sometime in the future. It is referenced, however, in the multiple endnotes that accompany each chapter, including references to the multiple oral interviews conducted in the early part of 2006 by Tim Christison or by the author. In alphabetical order, these were with:

Dave Armstrong

Ken Bendiktsen

Ron Bond

Fin Campbell

Bill Cochrane

Don Detomasi

Bob Dewar

Joyce Doolitttle,

Quentin Doolittle

Max Foran

Marsha Hanen

John Heintz

Ernie Ingles

John McLaren

Roger Jackson

Vern Jones

Jane Kelley

Gary Krivy

Peter Krueger

Alan MacDonald

Mike McMordie

Matt Mohtadi

Gordon Nelson

Terry Penelhum

Bill Perks

Jan Roseneder

Bob Schulz

Bob Sivertsen

Polly Steele

Bob Stebbins

Fred Terentiuk

Mary Valentich

Joan van Housen

Cathy Wagner

Bob Weyant

Matthew Zachariah

Additionally, several individuals chose e-mail as their form of response to the call for reminiscences, and they are included where applicable in the text. There are also the interviews in the university archives done in 1990 by Robert Bott for the 25th anniversary book, *A Place of Vision*, some of which are referenced and quoted within the footnotes.

This book is also based on primary sources the Calgary City Archives, the Glenbow Archives, and the University of Calgary Archives and Special Collections. For the early history in particular, the Provincial Archives of Alberta, and the University of Alberta Archives proved useful. The richest sources – getting richer yearly – are the University Archives, which contain not only the official record of the university in its several parts, but also some private correspondence such as the Andrew Doucette and Herbert Armstrong Papers from their years as the institution's head officers. Some private collections such as those of Ethel King-Shaw, George Self, and Helen Stadelbauer were also valuable. The newspaper records in the city and the university also provided a timeline and context for this narrative.

The best single history on the origins of the university is Robert M. Stamp's history of the Calgary Normal School and Faculty of Education, *Becoming a Teacher in 20th Century Calgary.* Other helpful histories of the early university are Norman Macleod's groundbreaking thesis on the early failure of Calgary College before World War I, and Phyllis E. Weston, "A University for Calgary," in the *Alberta Historical Review,* 1963, which are both cited within. Another deserving mention is Gloria Dalton's "1945-66: The Impatient Years," CALUM 8, no. 1 (December 1976).

In the recent past, significant research has been done by Harry Sanders and Donald Smith in preparing the ground for a scholarly history. Rob K. Omura's unpublished paper, "A Brief History of the University of Calgary, 1906–95" was done for me in 1995. And two titles to emerge very recently have been Harry Hiller's compilation of the Sociology Department's history, *First Forty* (2003), and Alan Robertson's personal memoir, partially on the university years when he was Director of Com Media and then Dean of Fine Arts, entitled *Those Who Can* (2006). Also, two excellent faculty histories deserve mention: first, Peter Glockner's *A Place of Ingenuity* (1994) on the history of engineering, and Geertje Boschma's *Faculty of Nursing on the Move* (2004), both of which have appeared in the last decade. Other histories are in the works – notably of the Department of Chemistry (Peter Krueger), and the Arctic Institute (Robert MacDonald), – so the shape of the past is becoming clearer with every passing decade.

SENIOR ACADEMIC OFFICERS OF THE UNIVERSITY OF CALGARY 1966–2006

PRESIDENTS

Herbert (Herb) Armstrong	1964–68
A.W.R. (Fred) Carrothers	1968–74
W.A. (Bill) Cochrane	1974–78
Norman (Norm) Wagner	1978–1988
Murray Fraser	1988–96
Terrence (Terry) White	1996–2001
Harvey P. Weingarten	2001–

VICE-PRESIDENTS (ACADEMIC)

Walter Trost	1966–68
James Cragg	1968–71
Finley Campbell	1971–76
Peter Krueger	1976–85, 1985–90
Peter Craigie	1985
Joy Calkin	1990–96
Ronald Bond	1996–2006
Alan Harrison	2006–

DEANS OF FACULTIES

Education   *1966–2006*

Howard Baker
John Macdonald
Robert Lawson
Frank Oliva

Ian Winchester
Annette LaGrange

Continuing Education   *1966–2006*
Division- Director- Fred Terentiuk (1966–76)
Stan Chapman
Bruce Hamilton
David Kirby
Tom Keenan
John Humphrey

School/Faculty of Physical Education/Kinesiology   *1961–2006*
Lou Goodwin
Roger Jackson
Warren Veale
Ron Zernicke
Wayne Giles

Graduate Studies   *1966–2006*
James B. Hyne
David Bercuson
Brian Gaines
Robert Mansell
Warren Veale

Arts and Science   *1966–75*
Terry Penelhum
Brian Wilson
Robert Wright
Robert Weyant

Humanities   *1976–2006*
John Woods
Peter Craigie
Brian Chellas
Ronald Bond
Hermina Joldersma (Acting)
John Humphrey (Acting)
Pierre Yves Moquais

Social Sciences   *1976–2006*
Horst Betz
Donald Seastone
Anthony Rasporich
Stephen Randall

Science   *1976–2006*
Neville Parsons
Tom Oliver
David Armstrong
John Kendall
Michael Boorman
J.S. Murphree

University College/General Studies/Communications and Culture 1976–2006
Fred Terentiuk, (Provost)
Robert Weyant
Marsha Hanen
Michael McMordie
Beverly Rasporich (Acting)
Kathleen Scherf

Engineering   *1966–2006*
AM. (Adam) Neville
R.A. (Bob) Ritter
T.H. (Tom) Barton
L.T. (Len) Bruton
E. (Ted) Rhodes
Chan Wirashinge
Elizabeth Cannon

Fine Arts   *1968–2006*
Fred Terentiuk (Acting)
A.R. Johnson
J.M. Salmon
Richard Johnson
Alan Robertson
Bernard Sheehan (Acting)
John Roberts

Maurice Yacowar
Ann Calvert

Medicine 1967–2006
William Cochrane
Lionel MacLeod
Mamoru Watanabe
Eldon Smith
Grant Gall

School/Faculty of Nursing 1969–2006
Shirley Good
Fred Terentiuk (Acting)
Marguerite Schumacher
Margaret Scott Wright
Janet Storch
Carol Rogers (Acting)
Deborah Tamblyn
Florence Myrick (Acting)
Marlene Reimer (Acting)
Michael Clinton

Social Work
F.H. (Tim) Tyler
Al Comanor (Acting)
Len Richards
Ray Tomlinson
Mary Valentich (Acting)
M.K. Zapf (Acting)
Gayla Rogers

Environmental Design 1972–2006
W.T. Bill Perks
Don Detomasi
Doug Gillmour (Acting)
Robert J.D. Page
M.E. Tyler
B.R. Sinclair

Law   *1974–2006*
John McLaren
Margaret Hughes
Constance Hunt
Sheila Martin
M.I. Wylie
Patricia Hughes